ELECTRONIC SECURITY SYSTEMS

by Leo G. Sands

THEODORE AUDEL & CO.
a division of

HOWARD W. SAMS & CO., INC.
4300 West 62nd Street
Indianapolis, Indiana 46268

FIRST EDITION

FIRST PRINTING—1973

International Standard Book Number: 0-672-23205-7
Library of Congress Catalog Card Number: 73-85724

FOREWORD

With burglary insurance rates skyrocketing—and even becoming unavailable in some area—and with the spiraling increase
in thefts during the past few years, a demand for information about
security systems has developed and the security equipment business
is booming.

This book was written in response to the high interest in security systems. It was written for electricians, electronics technicians,
security directors, and for do-it-yourself householders and businessmen.

Prior knowledge of electronics is not required to understand
most of this book since the functions and applications of the
various security device components are explained in easy-to-under-
stand language. Many alarm, control, detection, and surveillance
systems are described in detail. The last chapter states the criteria
for security system design and describes system installation and
maintenance practices.

LEO G. SANDS

CONTENTS

CHAPTER 1

Scope and Application
of Security Systems

Locking the barn door before the horse is stolen is a security precaution. So is removing the ignition key, rolling up the windows, and locking the doors when parking a vehicle; and locking the windows and doors of a house, apartment, or other building. Many insurance companies will not pay for stolen goods unless forced entry into a building is proved. Since most locks can be picked or opened with duplicate keys, tighter security measures are often required.

INTRUSION

Many commercial and residential buildings are equipped with local intrusion alarm systems. (See Fig. 1.) When a door or window is opened or broken, after the alarm system has been turned on, a bell, siren or other alerting device is automatically activated. Most such systems are triggered by one of several electrical switches or by breaking a metal foil strip that has been adhesively attached to a window. Others use a radar, ultrasonic or other type of electronic sensor which senses the presence or movements of persons within a protected area.

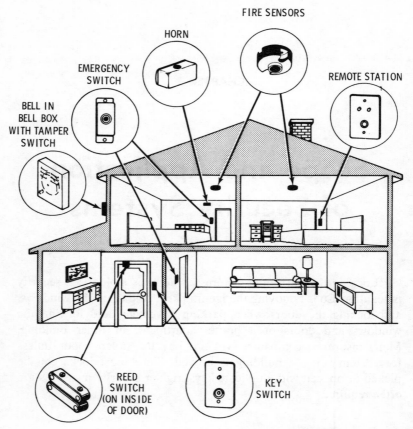

FIRE SENSORS

HORN

EMERGENCY
SWITCH

REMOTE STATION

BELL IN
BELL BOX
WITH TAMPER
SWITCH

REED
SWITCH
(ON INSIDE
OF DOOR)

KEY
SWITCH

Courtesy Electronic Instrument Co., Inc.

Fig. 1. Example of a fire and intrusion alarm system for a home.

FIRE ALARMS

Local fire alarm systems utilize temperature-sensing devices which trigger an alarm. Some of these sensors are quite sophisticated while others may be as simple as a pair of electrical contacts, under spring tension, separated by a chemical that melts at a high temperature and allows the contacts to mate and activate the alarm.

CENTRAL STATION ALARM SYSTEMS

In many communities, premises protection firms provide central station alarm service. The intrusion and/or fire sensors at a protected premises are connected to the central station through a "dedicated" wire line circuit which is usually leased from the local telephone company. A large number of premises can be protected and individually identified by such a system. When a sensor at a protected premises is tripped, an alarm at the central station is activated. This is followed by central station personnel telephoning the police, fire, or sheriff's department, as is appropriate, requesting emergency assistance.

In lieu of a dedicated wire-line circuit, central station alarm signals are being transmitted in some communities over CATV (cable television) cables. A central station alarm system can monitor all of the protected premises continuously or during specified hours, or interrogate each protected premises at frequent intervals, manually or automatically.

AUTOMATIC TELEPHONE DIALERS

Thousands of business establishments are equipped with an automatic telephone dialer which can be activated by a push button, intrusion or fire sensor, or by pushing a button on a pocket size radio or ultrasonic transmitter. The machine then automatically dials the number of the police department or a person responsible for the security of the establishment. After the called party replies, the machine transmits a tape-recorded announcement of the address of the establishment.

In most communities, the police will usually respond to an automatically dialed call for assistance. However, in some large cities, the police are reluctant or unwilling to respond to such calls, particularly if they have experienced a large number of false alarms.

Because of the large number of false fire alarms transmitted from conventional street-side fire alarm boxes, the City of New York is replacing conventional fire alarm boxes with new combination fire/police types which enable the responding agency to

9

engage in two-way voice communication with the person seeking emergency assistance. This is expected to cut down the number of false alarms.

ROADSIDE CALL BOXES

Call boxes are also being installed along major highways in the United States, West Germany, the Netherlands, and elsewhere to enable motorists to call for assistance by pushing buttons or by using voice communication. Some roadside call boxes contain radio transmitters (for one-way push-button signaling) or radio transceivers (for two-way voice communication). Other roadside call boxes are connected to an emergency dispatcher's office through telephone wires or coaxial cable.

CLOSED CIRCUIT TELEVISION

Closed circuit television (CCTV) systems are widely used for surveillance of buildings, open areas, and city streets. Such a system can consist of only one television camera and one video monitor (similar to a television receiver but without facilities for picking up television broadcast stations) interconnected through coaxial cable or, over short distances, through a telephone circuit. More elaborate CCTV systems employ more cameras and/or monitors and even video tape recorders (VTR).

Many apartment and office buildings employ CCTV to observe persons at building entrances and in elevators and garages. (See Fig. 2.) The cost of CCTV equipment has come down sufficiently to make it economically feasible for householders to install their own CCTV systems.

In Detroit, CCTV is being used to observe traffic on expressways, and in New York City, to observe activities in potentially high crime areas. The New York Police Department has a helicopter equipped with television cameras for observation of almost any area within the city. The television pictures are transmitted by microwave radio to a ground-based receiving station and then through cable to monitors at police headquarters.

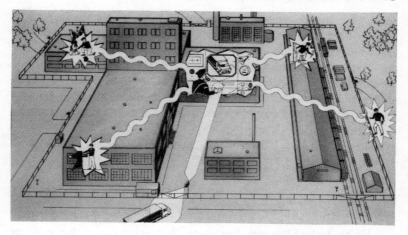

Courtesy Minneapolis-Honeywell Regulator Co.

Fig. 2. Artists concept of a centralized security system at an industrial complex which can be supervised by only two security guards.

AURAL SURVEILLANCE

"Bugs" for eavesdropping on private conversations are being used illegally by unauthorized persons. They are also being used legally by law enforcement officers. A bug may be a very compact radio transmitter or a microphone connected through wires to a listening device. Telephones can be modified so they will pick up sounds in a room without the occupants being aware that their conversations can be heard by others at distant locations. Of course, this is unlawful except when specifically authorized by court order.

Aural surveillance is also used for other than intentionally listening to private conversations. In buildings during hours when they are not supposed to be occupied by persons, microphones can be used to pick up the sounds of persons entering, leaving or moving about, the movement of vehicles and/or merchandise, etc.

HAZARD DETECTION

Sensors are used for detecting abnormal conditions, such as change in steam pressure, water seepage, excessive change in the

11

level of a liquid, presence of dangerous gases, etc. Such sensors transmit warning signals (via wire or radio) to a point where the information is needed. The signals can represent quantitative or qualitative information. An example of such a system is one used by a railroad to detect a significant rise in the level of a river under a bridge. When the water level rises above a specific level, a radio signal is transmitted which warns the crews (of approaching trains) of possible hazardous conditions. Many railroads have installed "hot box" (overheated bearing) detectors which control light signals or transmit a radio signal to the train containing a car with a hot box.

SECURE COMMUNICATION

Voice scramblers are becoming increasingly popular and are used for making telephone and radio conversations unintelligible. A combination scrambler/unscrambler connected or coupled to a telephone enables secure communication with a person at a similarly equipped telephone. Devices which accomplish the same purposes are also used in two-way mobile radio systems for transmission of messages not intended for interception by unauthorized persons. The use of voice scramblers in two-way radio systems is restricted by the Federal Communications Commission (FCC).

ACCESS CONTROL

Access to many buildings and fenced-in areas is controlled by devices into which an ID (identification) card is inserted which automatically unlocks a door or gate. Some doors and gates have electrically controlled locks which can be opened by dialing a specified number with a telephone dial or by pushing the buttons of a Touchtone encoder. Doors and gates are also locked and unlocked from remote locations with a push button or switch. The person controlling the door uses a telephone and on some models can actually see the television image of the person seeking entry.

Radio-equipped cars and trucks can be equipped with encoders to facilitate opening of doors and gates without the driver having to leave the vehicle.

ALERTING SYSTEMS

Security personnel can be alerted over a one-way paging system. Special tone signals can be transmitted over a loudspeaker paging system. Or each security officer can be furnished a pocket paging receiver which sounds a "beep" when he or she is being called and when an all-call emergency signal is transmitted. The receiver contains a decoder which is responsive only to one or more specially coded signals. These signals are broadcast by a radio transmitter (when radio paging is used) or radiated by a cable energized by a high-power audio amplifier (when inductive paging is used).

Some radio paging systems are equipped for signal-plus-voice transmission. First, a coded signal is transmitted to alert one or more persons. After the coded signal has been transmitted, a voice message is transmitted which is heard only by those whose paging receivers have been signalled.

Volunteer and off-duty police, fire, and civil defense officers in many areas are alerted in their homes and/or automobiles by coded radio signals. An officer has a radio receiver in his home and/or car which is tuned to a radio communications station and left turned on continuously. It remains mute, however, until the officer's own code or an all-call code is transmitted. It then sounds a beep and, optionally, a voice message. A lamp is also lighted which remains lit until extinguished by pushing a reset button.

PUBLIC PARTICIPATION

Thousands of persons who drive two-way radio-equipped vehicles participate in the *Community Radio Watch* program (CRW). When a CRW participant witnesses an accident, sees a crime in progress, or observes suspicious persons, he or she uses the two-way radio to report the facts to the dispatcher who, in turn, telephones the police.

In addition to CRW participants, several million CB operators (citizens band radio) who have two-way CB radios in their vehicles,

13

homes and/or offices, occasionally or regularly monitor CB Channel 9, the officially designated emergency channel, to listen for calls for assistance or information from motorists and householders. When a CB operator intercepts an emergency call, he or she lends direct assistance or notifies a law enforcement agency.

Countless people, particularly housewives, have monitor receivers for intercepting police, fire, and marine radio transmissions. While some police departments frown on public interception of their radio transmissions, many welcome it because listeners often call in to furnish information that may be of value to the police.

Many monitor receiver owners also listen in on the marine safety and calling channel (Channel 16) for distress calls from pleasure craft and commercial vessels. Persons who intercept such calls generally contact the Coast Guard or other public safety agency.

PERSONAL SECURITY

Many persons now take a CB (citizens band) walkie-talkie with them and use it when calling for assistance or reporting a crime or accident. Since the approximately 900,000 Citizens Radio Service licensees operate some 4,000,000 two-way radios, there are many who could intercept calls from persons in distress, particularly in highly populous areas.

The most positive way to obtain assistance or to report a crime or accident is to use a telephone to call the police or sheriff's department. In many communities, it is only necessary to dial "911" to reach the cognizant dispatcher in the area. Many street-side pay telephone stations can be used for dialing 911 without first having to insert a coin(s) in the telephone.

CHAPTER 2

Switches and Relays

Security alarm and control systems depend on switches to control the flow of electric current. These switches may be mechanical, electromagnetic, or electronic. The mechanical and electromagnetic switches employ moving parts. Electronic switches, on the other hand, have no moving parts. In this chapter, however, the functioning of electronic switches is often explained by showing conventional mechanical switches as the triggering devices. In actual security system applications, electronic switches can be triggered by mechanically actuated contacts or by application of an electrical potential. In many of the circuits shown in this chapter, a resistor is shown as a load. In practice, the load could be a lamp, motor, bell actuator, or other electrical device. Also in this chapter, discussion is limited to on-off switching as opposed to resistance variation which is covered in the next chapters.

MECHANICAL SWITCHES

The function of a switch is to control the flow of electric current. The most commonly used types of switches have normally open (NO) contacts. In the OFF position, the contacts are open and no current flows through the switch. In the ON position, the contacts are closed (touch each other) to allow current to flow through the switch. A conventional wall switch for turning electric lights on and off is known as NO contacts. A door bell push button is also an SPST switch with NO contacts. It differs from the wall switch in that its contact will automatically open when pressure on the button is released.

The schematic symbols for SPST NO switches are shown in Fig. 1. Symbols for SPST switches with normally closed (NC)

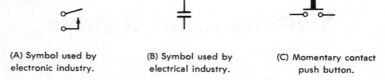

(A) Symbol used by electronic industry.

(B) Symbol used by electrical industry.

(C) Momentary contact push button.

Fig. 1. Symbols for normally open SPST switches.

contacts, are shown in Fig. 2. Normally, the contacts are closed to allow current in one device to cut off current flow in some other device. Fig. 2 A is the one used by the electronics industry.

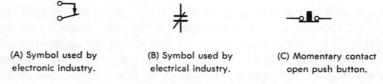

(A) Symbol used by electronic industry.

(B) Symbol used by electrical industry.

(C) Momentary contact open push button.

Fig. 2. Symbols for normally closed SPST switches.

Fig. 2 B is used by the electrical industry. The slanted line through the parallel lines indicates that the contacts are normally closed. Fig. 2 C is that of an SPST push button with NC contacts. Pushing the button opens the circuit. Releasing pressure on the button recloses the circuit.

A single-pole double-throw (SPDT) switch has both NO and NC contacts. Such a switch is used to transfer the flow of electric current from one circuit or device to another. Symbols for SPDT switches are shown in Fig. 3. Again, Fig. 3A is the electronics industry symbol, Fig. 3B is the electrical industry symbol, and

16

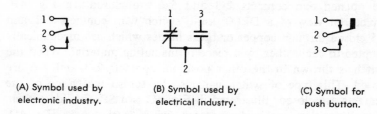

(A) Symbol used by electronic industry.

(B) Symbol used by electrical industry.

(C) Symbol for push button.

Fig. 3. Symbols for SPDT switches with one set of contacts normally closed.

Fig. 3C is the push-button symbol. In all three symbols it is indicated that contacts 1 and 2 are closed and contacts 2 and 3 are open in the normal position. When the switch is actuated, contacts 1 and 2 open and contacts 2 and 3 close.

A double-pole double-throw (DPDT) switch consists of two SPDT switches, as shown schematically in Fig. 4. In Fig. 4A are

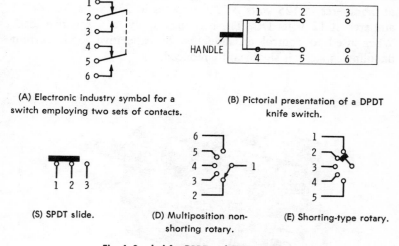

(A) Electronic industry symbol for a switch employing two sets of contacts.

(B) Pictorial presentation of a DPDT knife switch.

(S) SPDT slide.

(D) Multiposition non-shorting rotary.

(E) Shorting-type rotary.

Fig. 4. Symbol for DPDT and SPDT switches.

two **SPDT** switches whose armatures (moving contacts) are mechanically coupled (indicated by the dotted line). In the normal position, contacts 1-2 and 4-5 are closed and contacts 2-3 and 5-6 are open. When the switch is actuated, contacts 1-2 and 4-5

17

are opened and contacts 2-3 and 5-6 are closed. In Fig. 4B, a pictorial view of a DPDT knife switch with contacts 1-2 and 4-5 closed through copper or brass blades which are mechanically coupled to each other by a piece of insulating material. When the switch is thrown in the other position, contacts 2-3 and 5-6 are closed. This type of switch can also be set so that none of the contacts are closed. Illustrated in Fig. 4C is a SPDT slide switch. A multiposition nonshorting rotary switch is shown in Fig. 4D, and a shorting-type rotary switch is shown in Fig. 4E.

There are many other switch-contact configurations and combinations. A simple switch may control only one function whereas a complex switch assembly can control numerous circuits.

Ratings

Switch contacts are rated in terms of current-carrying capacity at a specified voltage. A typical toggle switch, for example, is rated at 6 amperes at 125 volts AC, 3 amperes at 250 volts AC, or 12 amperes at 12 volts DC. These ratings apply to a *resistive* load. When used to control an inductive or capacitive load, current handling capacity is significantly reduced.

Courtesy Cherry Electrical Products Corp.

Fig. 5. Pressure-contact switch.

Sensing

Either or both NO and NC contact switches are used in security systems to sense a change in the status of a circuit. Shown in Fig. 5 is a pressure-contact switch. Such a switch is used to sense the status of windows and doors. For example, when used with a casement window, pressure is applied to the plunger causing the NO contacts within the switch assembly to be closed. When the window is opened, pressure is released and the contacts open, thus

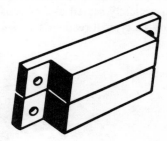

Fig. 6. A magnetic reed switch assembly.

triggering the alarm system. Alternately, the switch can be used where the NC set of contacts is held open by the plunger, and allowed to close when the window or door is opened.

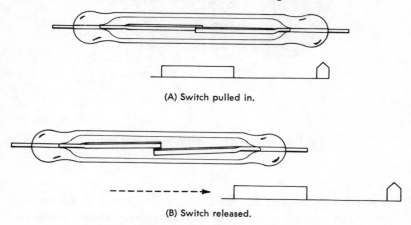

(A) Switch pulled in.

(B) Switch released.

Fig. 7. The function of a magnetic reed switch.

19

A magnetic reed switch is shown in Fig. 6. It consists of two units, one containing a bar magnet, the other containing a reed switch. When the two units are adjacent to each other as shown in Fig. 7A, the magnet causes the NO contacts of the reed switch to close. When the two units are separated, as shown in Fig. 7B, the magnetic field is removed and the contacts of the reed switch open.

A reed switch consists of a fixed contact and a moving contact arm which is pulled toward the fixed contact when the hermetically sealed assembly is exposed to a magnetic field. Fig. 8 shows a typical reed switch.

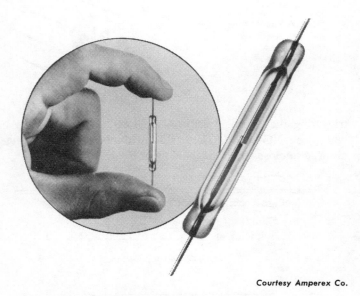

Courtesy Amperex Co.

Fig. 8. Examples of a hermetically sealed reed switch.

RELAYS

A relay is an electromagnetic switch. It consists of an electromagnet, an armature, and a switch assembly. When an electric current flows through the coil of the electromagnet, the armature "pulls in" and moves the contacts from their normal position to their energized position as shown in Fig. 9. When current through the coil is cut off, the relay "drops out", as shown in Fig. 9B.

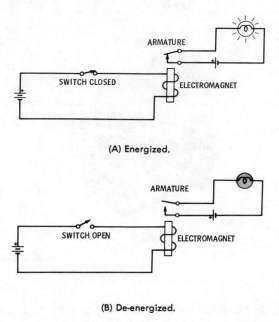

(A) Energized.

(B) De-energized.

Fig. 9. Simple relay circuit.

Fig. 10 is a photograph of a typical commercial relay with a four-pole double-throw (4PDT) contact assembly.

There are numerous relay contact configurations, including Form A (NO), Form B (NC), and Form C (DT), singly or stacked. A relay with DPDT Form C contacts, for example, can be used to transfer two independent circuits. Where high reliability is required, various means of connecting the relay contacts can be used. An example is shown in Fig. 11.

In Fig. 11A, the relay with 4PDT Form C contacts is used to control lamps *I1* and *I2*. When relay control switch *S* is open, the relay is not energized and lamp *I1* is on, obtaining its power from battery *B1*. Electron current flows through contacts 4, 5, 2, and

21

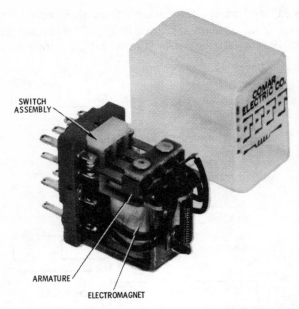

Fig. 10. A typical 4PDT relay.

1, and lamp *I1*. Electron current also flows through contacts 11, 10, 8, and 7. This hookup provides redundancy—two paths. If contacts 1-2 should fail to mate properly, current will flow through contacts 7-8, or vice versa. The same is true of contacts 4-5 with respect to contacts 10-11.

When switch *S* is closed, the relay pulls in causing contacts 1-2, 4-5, 7-8, and 10-11 to open and contacts 2-3, 5-6, 8-9, and 11-12 to close. Lamp *I1* goes out and lamp *I2* is energized by battery *B2*. Electron current flows through contacts 12, 11, 8, and 9. Electron current also flows through contacts 5, 6, 2, and 3 to provide redundancy. Failure of contacts 11-12 to mate properly will not prevent current flow since these contacts are backed up by contacts 5-6. The same is true of contacts 8-9 with respect to contacts 2-3. Such an elaborate switching circuit is not commonly used, but is shown here to illustrate capability.

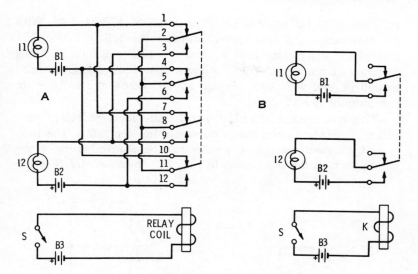

Fig. 11. An example of a contact redundancy circuit is shown in figure A. The same function can be performed by the circuit shown in figure B but with lower reliability.

Ratings

Relays are rated in terms of sensitivity, current switching capacity, operate (pull-in) time, release (drop-out) time, and vibration/shock resistance. Most relays are designed to be energized by DC at voltages ranging from 6 to 110 volts. The armature is pulled in when the ampere-turns is adequate to overcome the inertia of the armature and the mechanical load of the switch assembly. After being pulled in, the armature will not release until the ampere-turns is sufficiently reduced. The strength of the magnetic field (ampere-turns) of an electromagnet depends on the product of current and the number of coil turns.

Relays, however, are not rated in terms of ampere-turns but instead in terms of coil resistance and current. For example, a typical DPDT general purpose relay with a 470-ohm coil (DC resistance of winding) will pull in when coil current is 0.018 ampere (18 mA) or greater. The particular relay in question is rated as a 24-volt relay. However, it will pull in with only 8.5

23

volts across its coil since $E = IR$ or $0.018 \times 470 = 8.46$. With 24 volts across the coil, current through the coil will be 0.051 ampere (51 mA), since $I = E/R$ or $24/470 = 0.051$. In terms of power, a minimum of 153 milliwatts is required for the relay to pull in, and with rated voltage applied across the coil, power consumption is 1.22 watts.

The coil resistance and power requirements of relays vary widely, depending upon the power switching capability. The pull-in and drop-out voltage of a relay can be checked using a test circuit such as the one shown in Fig. 12. Potentiometer R is ad-

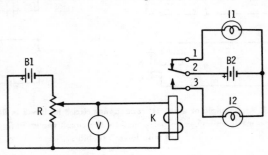

Fig. 12. Relay test circuit.

justed from its 0 volts position until lamp $I2$ lights, denoting that the relay has pulled in. The voltmeter indication is then noted. The potentiometer is now adjusted to lower the coil voltage until lamp $I1$ lights, denoting that the relay has released. The voltmeter reading is again noted.

Response

The operating (pull-in) time of conventional relays is several milliseconds. Where faster response and greater sensitivity are required, reed relays are often used. The operating time of a reed relay can be as low as 1 millisecond and release time only 0.5 millisecond.

Some relays are designed for slow-actuate or slow-release. The operate and release time of a conventional relay can be increased by connecting a capacitor and a resistor in the coil circuit, as

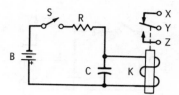

Fig. 13. Slow-actuate, slow-release relay circuit.

shown in Fig. 13. When switch S is first closed, capacitor C looks like a short circuit across the relay coil. As the capacitor charges through resistor R, the voltage across the relay coil rises. When this voltage is high enough, the relay pulls in. When switch S is opened, the relay remains energized until the charge in C falls below the release voltage of the relay.

In some applications, the relay should pull in quickly and then drop out. This can be done by using the circuit shown in Fig. 14.

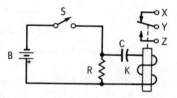

Fig. 14. Momentary-operated relay circuit.

When switch S is first closed, full battery voltage reaches the relay coil. As capacitor C charges through the relay coil, the voltage across the relay coil falls and the relay armature is released. When switch S is opened, C discharges through resistor R.

AC-Operated

Relays are available which are designed to operate on AC. They require more operating power than equivalent DC relays and are often noisier. It is common practice to use DC relays in AC circuits. This can be done by rectifying the AC as shown in Fig. 15. In Fig. 15A, diode $CR1$ serves as a half-wave series rectifier; capacitor C serves as a filter to prevent relay chatter and increase the level of the DC voltage. Diode CR in Fig. 15B is used as a half-wave shunt rectifier in conjunction with capacitor C. In Fig. 15C, four diodes are used in a full-wave bridge rectifier circuit.

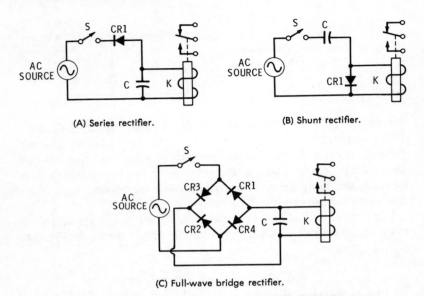

(A) Series rectifier.

(B) Shunt rectifier.

(C) Full-wave bridge rectifier.

Fig. 15. Circuits for operation of a DC relay from an AC power source.

The *Alco* FR-101 isolation relay is designed to be energized by AC. As shown in Fig. 16, it has three windings and a pair of NO contacts. The AC supply voltage is applied across primary

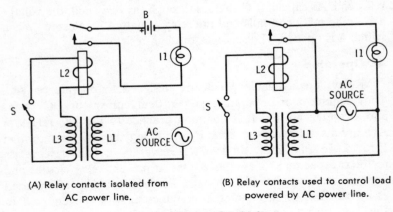

(A) Relay contacts isolated from AC power line.

(B) Relay contacts used to control load powered by AC power line.

Fig. 16. Isolation relay circuits.

winding *L1*. The contacts will not close until windings *L2* and *L3* (in series) are shorted by switch *S*. The voltage and current in the *L2-L3* loops are low and are isolated from the AC power line—a safety feature. The contacts can be used to control an isolated circuit, as shown in Fig. 16A, or to control a lamp or other device energized by the AC power line, as shown in Fig. 16B.

SEMICONDUCTOR ELECTRONIC SWITCHES

In addition to being used as rectifiers, diodes are also used as electronic switches, particularly in logic circuits. A very simple diode circuit is shown in Fig. 17. No current will flow through

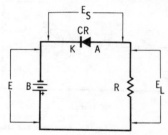

Fig. 17. Diode switch demonstration circuit.

the circuit unless the applied DC voltage (E) is higher than the surface barrier voltage of diode *CR*. The diode acts as an open switch. If E is greater or somewhat less than 1 volt, current will flow through *CR* and load resistance *R*. For example, if E is 9 volts and *R* is 10 ohms, E_S (voltage drop across *CR*) will be about 0.6 volt (when *CR* is a silicon diode) and E_L (voltage across *R*) will be about 8.4 volts. If E is varied, E_L will vary but E_S will remain almost constant.

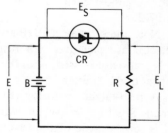

Fig. 18. Zener diode switch demonstration circuit.

27

In higher voltage circuits, an avalanche diode can be used which will not pass current until the applied voltage exceeds the avalance threshold of the diode.

A zener diode is used in the circuit shown in Fig. 18. No current flows through the circuit until the applied voltage E is greater than the zener voltage of CR. For example, if E is 12 volts, the zener voltage E_s of CR is 9.1 volts, E_L will be 2.9 volts. As E is varied, E_s will remain constant at 9.1 volts and E_L will vary. The zener diode functions as a voltage-controlled switch.

Bipolar transistors are also used as electronic switches. Demonstration circuits are shown in Fig. 19. In Fig. 19A, a PNP tran-

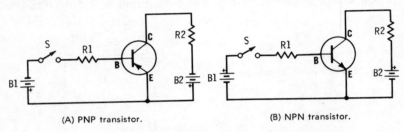

(A) PNP transistor.　　　　　　　(B) NPN transistor.

Fig. 19. Bipolar transistor switch demonstration circuit.

sistor is used and in Fig. 19B an NPN transistor is used. In either circuit, no current flows through load resistor $R2$ when switch S is open. When S is closed, the base of the transistor is forward biased by the voltage from battery $B1$, and base current flows through $R1$ which limits the current to prevent damage to the transistor. When the base current is adequately high, the transistor is "saturated" and the collector-to-emitter resistance of the transistor is almost zero, allowing maximum current to flow through load $R2$.

Note then, when a PNP transistor is used, both the base and collector are negative with respect to the emitter. And when an NPN transistor is used, both the base and collector are positive with respect to the emitter.

A field-effect transistor (FET) is shown in the demonstration circuit. See Fig. 20. When switch S is open, current through load $R3$ is low because of the reverse bias developed across $R2$ in the

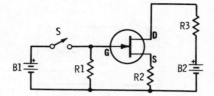

Fig. 20. Field effect transistor switch demonstration circuit.

source circuit of the FET. When S is closed, forward-bias voltage from battery *B1* offsets the reverse-bias voltage across *R2* and drain current through *R3* rises. Since an FET is quite fragile, use is limited to low power circuits.

A silicon controlled rectifier (SCR), a type of thyristor, is used as an electronic switch in the circuit shown in Fig. 21. When

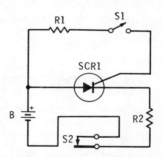

Fig. 21. Silicon controlled rectifier switch demonstration circuit.

switch *S1* is open, no current flows through the circuit. However, when *S1* is closed momentarily, a positive pulse is applied to the gate of the SCR and current flows through the circuit. The current flow cannot be stopped except by removing the DC supply voltage. In this example, current flow is stopped by momentarily opening the normally closed switch (*S2*). Thus, if *S1* and *S2* are push buttons, power can be applied by momentarily operating *S1* and turned off by momentarily operating *S2*.

When used in an AC circuit, as shown in Fig. 22, current flows during each half-cycle when the anode of the SCR is positive with respect to its cathode, but not during the other half-cycles. In this demonstration circuit, switch *S* must be closed continuously to cause load current to flow. The SCR is gated into conduction during each positive half-cycle of the AC supply voltage. It should

29

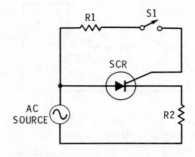

Fig. 22. SCR used as a switch in an AC circuit.

be noted that pulsating DC flows through the load when a single SCR is used in an AC circuit.

A diac, also a type of thyristor, performs somewhat the same function in an AC circuit as the diode in the DC circuit previously shown in Fig. 17. In the AC circuit shown in Fig. 23, the diac is

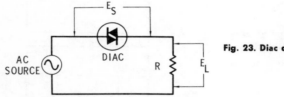

Fig. 23. Diac demonstration circuit.

in series with the load. No current flows through the circuit until the AC supply voltage exceeds approximately 35 volts. Then, current flows in both directions through the diac and the load. A diac, which has limited applications, can be used as a voltage-controlled switch.

The triac is a unique and valuable thyristor with numerous applications in AC circuits. In Fig. 24, the triac is used as a gated switch. No current flows through the circuit when switch S is open. When this switch is closed, a gating current flows through $R1$ which causes the triac to conduct during both half-cycles of the AC supply voltage. When a triac is used, S can be a switch or a pair of relay contacts which have to pass very little current to control much higher load current. For example, only 0.1 ampere (100 mA) of gating current is required to control 40 amperes of load current.

30

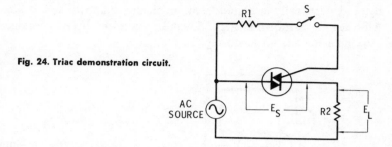

Fig. 24. Triac demonstration circuit.

ELECTRON TUBE SWITCHES

The thermionic diode vacuum tube in Fig. 25 performs somewhat the same function as the diode previously shown in Fig. 17.

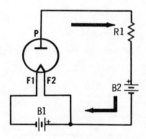

Fig. 25. Thermionic diode demonstration circuit.

The filament (cathode) of the diode tube is heated by the current furnished by battery *B1*. The plate (anode) is kept at a positive potential with respect to the cathode by battery *B2*. Electrons emitted by the cathode (filament) are attracted to the plate and provide a current path through the tube. The amount of current flowing through load *R* depends on the temperature of the cathode, the plate supply voltage (from *B2),* and the resistance of *R*. Unlike the semiconductor diode previously shown in Fig. 17, the voltage drop across the diode tube does not remain constant as supply voltage and load resistance vary.

The directly heated cathode (filament) type of tube is seldom used except in some high-voltage rectifier applications. Most elec-

31

tron tubes of all types employ a cathode which is indirectly heated by, and electrically insulated from, an electrode known as a heater. This heater, as shown in Fig. 26, can be energized by AC obtained through a stepdown transformer T.

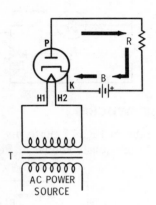

Fig. 26. Thermionic diode with indirectly heated cathode.

In the triode tube circuit shown in Fig. 27 and the pentode tube circuit shown in Fig. 28, the heater is not shown but it is

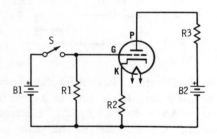

Fig. 27. Triode-tube switch demonstration circuit.

assumed that it exists. In a triode tube (Fig. 27), electrons flow from the heated cathode (K), through a wire electrode known as the grid (G) to the positively polarized plate (P). The amount of current flowing through load $R3$ is varied by the voltage applied to the grid.

When switch S is open, the grid is reverse-biased by the voltage drop across cathode resistor $R2$. This causes the grid (G) to be

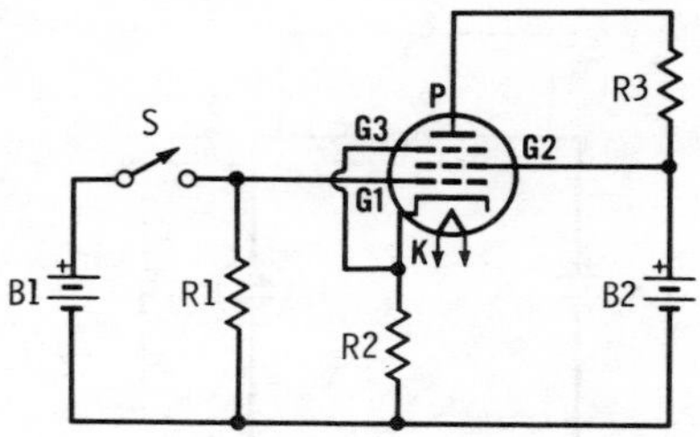

Fig. 28. Pentode-tube switch
demonstration circuit.

negative with respect to the cathode (K). The more negative the grid, the more electrons it repels back to the cathode and the lower the load current. When S is closed, a positive voltage from battery B1 is applied across R1 and to the grid. This positive voltage (always somewhat lower than the bias voltage across R2) reduces the reverse bias on the grid, allowing load current to rise as a result of reduction of the resistance of the plate-cathode path through the tube.

The pentode tube shown in Fig. 28 has three grids. G1 is the control grid, G2 is the screen grid, and G3 is the suppressor grid. Both the plate and the screen grid are kept at a positive potential with respect to the cathode by the plate supply battery (B2). The control grid is reverse-biased by the voltage drop across cathode resistor R2. When switch S is open, load current through R3 is low because of the reverse bias on G1. When S is closed, the positive potential from battery B2 offsets the reverse bias voltage and reduces the plate-cathode resistance allowing load current to increase.

GAS TUBES

The electrodes of conventional electron tubes are within a glass envelope from which the air and gases have been evacuated and, hence, are often called "vacuum tubes." The envelopes of some special purpose tubes contain a small amount of argon or other inert gas which can be ionized. The most common type of gas tube is the neon lamp which is often used as a status indicator. It is also used as a voltage regulator and as an electronic switch.

33

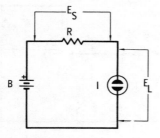

Fig. 29. Neon-lamp switch demonstration circuit.

Fig. 29 is a simple demonstration circuit. When the supply voltage from battery B is less than approximately 60 volts, current will not flow through the circuit. When the applied voltage is increased sufficiently, neon lamp I ionizes and emits a reddish-orange light. As the applied voltage is varied, voltage E_L across the lamp remains constant but voltage E_S across resistor R varies. The lamp exhibits negative-resistance characteristics — its resistance decreases as current through it increases. When the applied voltage is reduced to below approximately 40 volts, the lamp extinguishes and again becomes an open circuit. Neon lamps are useful as voltage-controlled switches in low-current applications.

The so-called "VR" tube is most commonly used as a voltage regulator but can also be used as a voltage-controlled electronic switch. It has characteristics similar to those of the zener diode discussed previously. As shown in Fig. 30, a VR tube has a plate

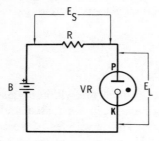

Fig. 30. VR-tube switch demonstration circuit.

(anode) and a cold cathode within a gas-filled glass envelope. Unlike the bidirectional neon lamp, the VR tube will conduct only when its plate is positive with respect to its cathode and only when the applied voltage exceeds the tube's ionization potential. VR tubes are commonly available in 75-, 90-, 105-, and 150-volt ratings and are capable of safely passing currents up to 0.03 ampere (30 mA).

Referring again to Fig. 30, assume that battery B furnishes 90 volts DC and the VR tube is rated at 105 volts. The tube will not ionize and current will not flow through the circuit. If the battery is replaced by one delivering 135 volts, the VR tube ionizes and current flows through the circuit. The voltage (E_L) across the VR tube will hold steady at 105 volts and voltage E_s across resistor R will be 30 volts but will vary as the applied voltage varies. Like a neon lamp, a VR tube has negative-resistance characteristics.

The thyratron tube is available as a triode or tetrode gas filled tube and with either a heated cathode or a cold cathode. Fig. 31

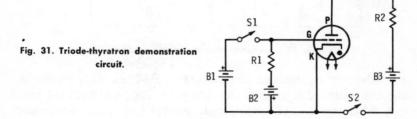

Fig. 31. Triode-thyratron demonstration circuit.

shows a thyratron triode with a heated cathode (heater not shown) in an electronic switch circuit. When switch $S1$ is open, the grid is reverse-biased by battery $B2$ to keep the grid sufficiently negative to prevent electron flow from the cathode to the plate. When $S1$ is closed momentarily, battery $B1$ applies a positive potential to the grid to offset the reverse bias. This causes the tube to ionize; the plate-cathode resistance becomes very low and maximum current flows through load $R2$.

Reopening $S1$ has no effect. Once ionized, the tube continues to conduct until the plate supply voltage is removed. This can be

35

done by momentarily opening normally closed switch *S2*. After *S2* is reclosed, the tube can again be turned on by momentarily closing *S1*. When the plate supply voltage is AC, load current flows during every half-cycle when *S1* is kept closed. The tube is automatically extinguished during the AC half-cycles where the plate is made negative with respect to the cathode.

A thyratron tetrode demonstration circuit is given in Fig. 32. In this example, the plate supply voltage is AC. This tube has two control grids (triggers), either of which can be used to trigger

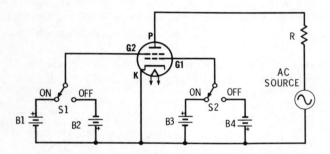

Fig. 32. Tetrode-thyratron demonstration circuit.

the tube into conduction. Switches *S1* and *S2* are both shown in the ON position. A positive DC voltage is applied to both *G1* and *G2*. Whenever the AC plate supply voltage makes the plate posi-

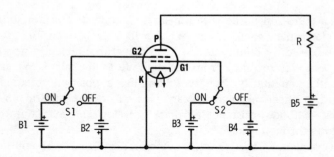

Fig. 33. Tetrode-thyratron demonstration circuit with DC power source.

36

tive with respect to the cathode, current (pulsating DC) flows through load *R*. Load current can be cut off by setting either *S1* or *S2* to the OFF position. Both must be in the ON position to cause load current to flow.

When the plate supply voltage is DC, as shown in Fig. 33, load current will start to flow when both *S1* and *S2* are set to the ON position. Load current will continue to flow when either or both *S1* and *S2* are set to the OFF position because the grids will have lost their control. They can only regain control by momentarily cutting off the plate supply voltage.

GATED-BEAM TUBE

The gated-beam tube (3BN6, 6BN6, 12BN6, etc.) is a unique electronic switch whose schematic symbol is the same as that of a conventional pentode tube. But, its characteristics are very different. As stated earlier, a pentode (Fig. 28) has three grids—control grid (*G1*), screen grid (*G2*), and suppressor grid (*G3*). A gated-beam tube as shown in Fig. 34, also has three grids—control grid

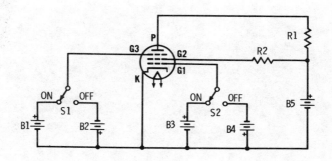

Fig. 34. Gated-beam tube demonstration circuit.

(*G1*), accelerator grid (*G2*), and quadrature grid (*G3*). In a pentode, *G3* voltage has very little effect on plate current. But, in a gated-beam tube, both *G1* and *G3* have almost equal effect on plate current.

In the diagram, both $G1$ and $G3$ are at a positive potential (forward biased)—both $S1$ and $S2$ are shown in the ON position. If the positive potential on these grids is at least 2 volts, the tube is saturated and maximum current flows through load R. Since this is not a gas-filled tube (e.g. a thyratron), the grids retain control. Load current can be cut off by setting either $S1$ or $S2$ to the OFF position to apply a reverse bias (negative) voltage to either $G1$ or $G2$.

SPECIAL PURPOSE SWITCHES

There are numerous types of switches including push buttons with built-in status indicator lamps and latched push-button switch assemblies with fairly complex contact configuration. An example of a complex switching assembly which is used for interconnecting any of its circuits to any of its other circuits is shown in Fig. 35. This is known as a crossbar switching system.

Courtesy James Cunningham, Son and Co.

Fig. 35. Push-button crossbar switch assembly.

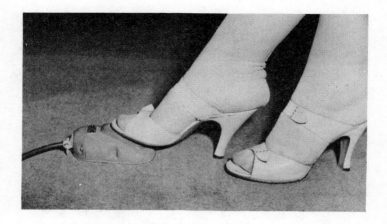

Fig. 36. Typical foot switch.

Fig. 37. Key lock switch.

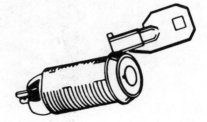

Courtesy Electronic Instrument Co., Inc.

The foot switch shown in Fig. 36 is used in security and communication system applications. For example, it can be used to actuate an alarm or activate a radio transmitter or tape recorder.

A commonly used security system component is a key-lock switch, such as the one shown in Fig. 37. This kind of switch is often used for disarming an alarm system.

When an intrusion alarm system is to be operational only during certain hours, clock-actuated switches, such as those shown in Fig. 38 may be employed. This particular clock-actuated switch can be set to turn an alarm system on and off at the same times on any selected days. More complex clocks are available which pro-

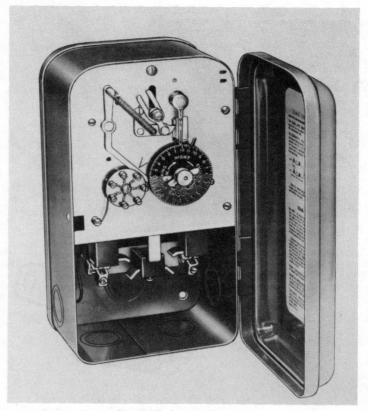

Fig. 38. Clock actuated switch.

vide several automatic operations per day, and which can change programs from day to day.

CHAPTER 3

Sensors and Encoders

A *sensor* is a device which senses a gradual or abrupt physical change and converts it into an electrical signal. When the NO contacts of a switch close, a digital "1" signal is transmitted. When the NC contacts of a switch open, a digital "0" signal is transmitted. Conversely, closing of NO contacts can represent an "0" digital signal and opening of NC contacts can represent a "1" digital signal. An example of a digital sensor is a thermostat or a window or door switch which has two possible contact states—open or closed.

An analog sensor, on the other hand, produces a proportional output signal. For example, the resistance of a photoelectric cell or photosensitive resistor varies with the intensity of the light it intercepts. The resistance of a thermistor reduces as the temperature it senses rises. The capacitance of an electrostatic pressure sensor rises with applied pressure. And the inductance of an inductive motion sensor rises or falls with motion excursion.

SENSOR SWITCHES

Mechanically actuated switches are used as sensors in numerous security applications to detect movement such as the opening of doors and windows. The switches shown in Fig. 1, for example,

(A) Lever type. (B) Roller leaf type.

Fig. 1. Examples of pressure-actuated snap-action SPDT switches.

have snap-action mechanisms that ensure firm contact. The one shown in Fig. 1A has a lever actuator which applies pressure to a button which in turn trips the mechanism. When used as a window-opening sensor, the lever would normally be depressed and opening the window would allow the lever pressure to be relaxed, allowing the switch to operate. The one shown in Fig. 1B is similar but has a roller at the end of its lever. Both of the particular switches shown here have SPDT contacts which can be used for opening or closing a circuit when pressure is removed from the lever.

The leaf contact switch shown in Fig. 2 was designed specifically for protecting casement and double-hung windows, sliding

Fig. 2. Leaf contact switch which opens the contacts when pressure is removed.

Courtesy Electronic Instrument Co., Inc.

doors, and screens. Its SPST contacts are closed when pressure is removed.

The door jamb switch shown in Fig. 3 has SPST NO contacts. When the door is closed, the contacts close and when the door is opened, the contacts open.

Fig. 3. Door jamb switch which opens
the contacts when door is opened.

Courtesy Electronic Instrument Co., Inc.

VIBRATION SENSORS

The compact vibration sensor shown in Fig. 4 can be attached
to a wall, ceiling, large glass window, skylight, safe, file cabinet

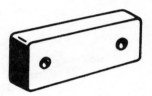

Fig. 4. Vibration sensor switch.

Courtesy Electronic Instrument Co., Inc.

or other flat surface. It can be adjusted to protect concrete block
surfaces up to five feet in any direction. When it senses vibration,
its NC SPST contacts open. Another example of a vibration sensor

Fig. 5. Pulsor walk detector which is
attached below a floor, roof, stair
steps or fire escape.

Courtesy Detectron Security Systems, Inc.

is the *Pulsor* (a trade name), shown in Fig. 5, which is attached
by means of epoxy under a floor, stair step, or roof.

43

PRESSURE SWITCHES

Switch-type sensors which respond to momentary pressure are shown in Fig. 6. The one shown in Fig. 6A is known as a ribbon switch that is sensitive to light pressure and which can be placed under a rug or other object. Pressure anywhere along its length, except at its extreme ends, causes momentary closure of its NO contacts. They are ¾ inch wide, ³⁄₁₆ inch thick, and available in 1-, 2-, or 5- foot lengths. Connections are made through 18-inch leads at one end.

The mat switch shown in Fig. 6B is widely used in front of doors and is actuated when a person steps on it. It consists of six parallel ribbon switches. Only five pounds of pressure is required to obtain contact closure. The foot switch shown in Fig. 6C can be taped or cemented to the floor.

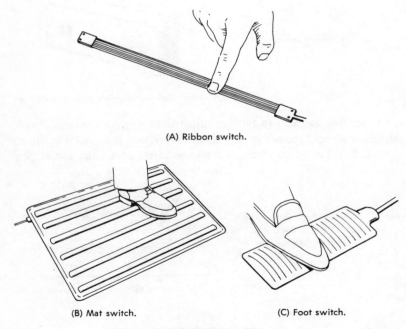

(A) Ribbon switch.

(B) Mat switch.   (C) Foot switch.

Fig. 6. Switch-type sensors.

Fig. 7. Pressure switch used to protect valuable objects. Lifting objects closes the circuit setting off the alarm.

The *Pilferage Sentinel* (a trade name), shown in Fig. 7, is intended for placement under a valuable stationary object such as a lamp, vase, TV set, etc., or under a filing cabinet or the legs of a piece of furniture. When the object is lifted, the switch contacts are actuated.

MAGNETIC SWITCHES

One of the most popular types of sensors is the magnetic reed switch, shown in Fig. 8, which consists of two parts. One part

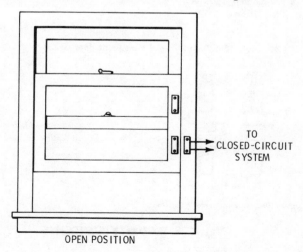

OPEN POSITION

Fig. 8. Magnetic window switch.

45

contains a permanent magnet and the other contains an NO reed switch. These magnetic reed switches are used mainly to protect doors and windows. When the two parts are side by side (vertically or horizontally), the magnet causes the NO contacts of the reed switch to be held closed. When separated, the switch contacts open.

An example of a door switch is shown in Fig. 9. When the door is closed, the switch contacts are closed, and when the door is opened, the switch contacts open.

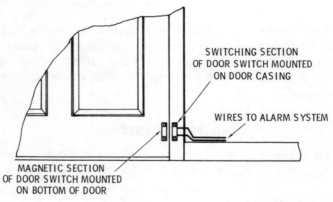

SWITCHING SECTION OF DOOR SWITCH MOUNTED ON DOOR CASING

WIRES TO ALARM SYSTEM

MAGNETIC SECTION OF DOOR SWITCH MOUNTED ON BOTTOM OF DOOR

Courtesy Teletronics, Inc.

Fig. 9. Example of a magnetic door switch.

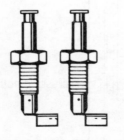

Fig. 10. Pin switches used in installation on auto doors.

Courtesy Electronic Instrument Co., Inc.

VEHICLE SECURITY SWITCHES

The pin switches shown in Fig. 10 are designed to be actuated by the opening of a door or the trunk or hood of an automobile.

The switch shown in Fig. 11 is actuated when one end of a vehicle is lifted by a tow truck or raised by a jack.

Courtesy Electronic Instrument Co., Inc.

TEMPERATURE SENSORS

The most common type of temperature sensor is the thermostat which opens its contacts when a specific temperature is reached and recloses its contacts when the temperature falls to a specific level. The thermostat may be designed so that it closes its contacts when temperature rises to a certain level and opens them when the temperature falls to a certain level. An example of a

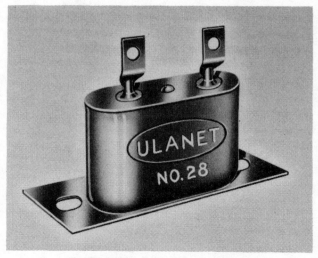

Fig. 12. Surface-mounted thermostat switch.

surface-mounted thermostat is shown in Fig. 12. It senses the temperature of the surface to which it is mounted.

The contacts of a conventional home-heating system thermostat open when a specific temperature is reached whereas the contacts of an air conditioner thermostat close when a specific temperature is reached. Either can be used as a fire sensor. The former can be used in a circuit in which the opening of the contacts actuates an alarm and the latter in a circuit which is actuated by contact closure. Of course, the temperature control dial should be set for a temperature higher than would be expected under ordinary circumstances.

A professional combination thermometer and thermostat is pictured in Fig. 13. Its dial indicates the ambient temperature. Its internal thermostat closes its NO contacts when the temperature rises to 100° F or falls to 45° F. In a security system application, this instrument can be used to sense the failure of a heating or air conditioning system, or as a fire alarm actuator.

Fig. 13. Combination thermometer and thermostat.

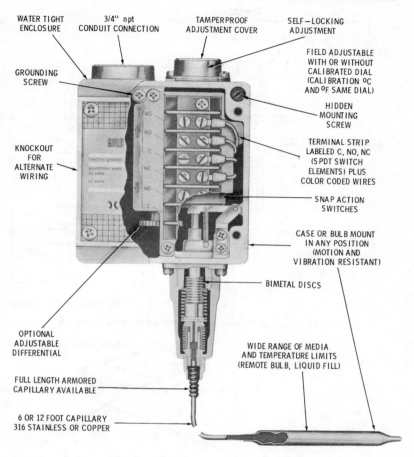

WATER TIGHT
ENCLOSURE

3/4" npt
CONDUIT CONNECTION

TAMPERPROOF
ADJUSTMENT COVER

SELF—LOCKING
ADJUSTMENT

FIELD ADJUSTABLE
WITH OR WITHOUT
CALIBRATED DIAL
(CALIBRATION °C
AND °F SAME DIAL)

GROUNDING
SCREW

HIDDEN
MOUNTING
SCREW

TERMINAL STRIP
LABELED C, NO, NC
(SPDT SWITCH
ELEMENTS) PLUS
COLOR CODED WIRES

KNOCKOUT
FOR
ALTERNATE
WIRING

SNAP ACTION
SWITCHES

CASE OR BULB MOUNT
IN ANY POSITION
(MOTION AND
VIBRATION RESISTANT)

BIMETAL DISCS

OPTIONAL
ADJUSTABLE
DIFFERENTIAL

WIDE RANGE OF MEDIA
AND TEMPERATURE LIMITS
(REMOTE BULB, LIQUID FILL)

FULL LENGTH ARMORED
CAPILLARY AVAILABLE

6 OR 12 FOOT CAPILLARY
316 STAINLESS OR COPPER

Courtesy Barksdale Controls

Fig. 14. Dual control temperature switch.

An example of a dual-temperature control switch is shown
in Fig. 14. Temperature is sensed by the remote bulb (lower right)
which is connected to the switch-controlling bellows through a 6-
or 12- foot capillary tube. The bulb can sense the temperature of
the air, a surface, or a liquid. The bellows controls two SPDT snap
action switches. Connections to the switch contacts are made at
screws on the built-in barrier terminal block.

49

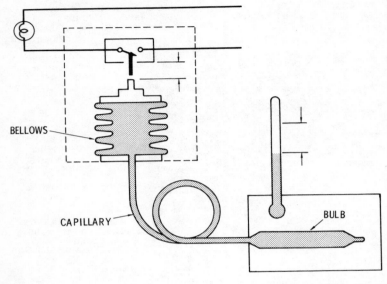

Courtesy Barksdale Controls

Fig. 15. Functional diagram of a liquid-filled temperature switch.

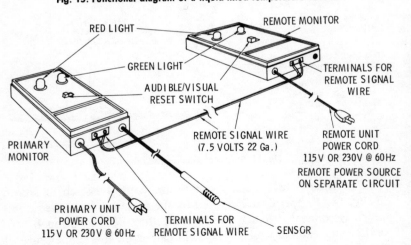

Courtesy Mack Electric Devices, Inc.

Fig. 16. Temperature monitor system with remote monitor.

Fig. 15 shows how the bellows is actuated by temperature sensed by the bulb. The bulb and capillary tube contain a liquid which expands with an increase in temperature and which increases the pressure on the bellows that controls the switch.

A temperature monitoring system is shown pictorially in Fig. 16. The unit at the left is the primary monitor and the one at the right is remote monitor. They can be up to ½ mile apart. The temperature sensor is connected to the primary monitor. When a dangerous temperature is sensed, the green lights (normal—condition indicators) on both monitors are extinguished and the red lights are automatically turned on. An audible alarm at each of the monitors is also actuated. The audible alarm can be silenced at either or both monitors but the red lights remain lit until the temperature returns to a safe level. Then the red lights go out and the green lights are turned on.

Courtesy Mack Electric Devices, Inc.

Fig. 17. Temperature sensor.

The temperature sensor is shown in Fig. 17. Within the stainless steel enclosure is a mercurial thermostat. The enclosure permits direct contact with the liquid or air being monitored without danger of damaging the thermostat.

Thermistors, which are available in various configurations, as shown in Fig. 18, are temperature-sensitive resistors and are widely used for sensing changes in temperature. The change in the resistance of a thermistor, caused by a change in temperature, is used in fire alarm systems to actuate an alarm. They are also used as liquid-level sensors. For example, a thermistor attached to a wall in a basement can be used to trigger an alarm when water rises as it contacts the thermistor, causing an abrupt change in its resistance.

Another crude but effective fire sensor consists of a pair of spring-loaded electrical contacts which are normally separated by paraffin or other easily melted substance. When the temperature

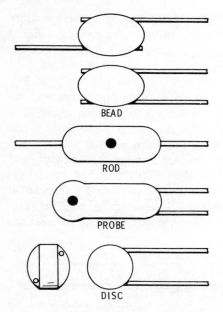

BEAD

ROD

Fig. 18. Examples of thermistors.

PROBE

DISC

rises high enough to melt the substance, the contacts are closed by spring pressure.

LIGHT SENSORS

There are several types of light-sensing devices including those which generate a voltage whose level rises with light intensity, light-sensitive diodes, transistors and the LASCR (light-actuated silicon controlled rectifier).

The earlist type is the vacuum or gas-filled photoelectric cell which is a cold-cathode electron tube whose electron emission is controlled by the intensity of the light impinging on its cathode. The greater the light intensity, the lower the anode-to-cathode resistance. Several newer types of photoconductive cells have been developed which are more sensitive and smaller. Examples of modern photoconductive cells are shown in Fig. 19.

How the change of resistance of a photoconductive cell is utilized is illustrated in Fig. 20. The cell, a resistance (R) and a

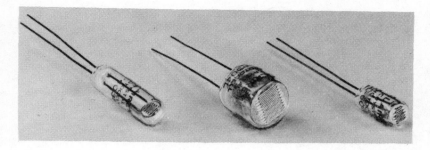

Courtesy Clairex Corp.

Fig. 19. Examples of photoconductive cells.

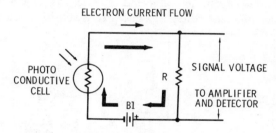

Fig. 20. Circuit employing a photoconductive cell.

battery are connected in series. With no light impinging on the cell, its resistance is high and the current through the circuit is low. Therefore, the voltage drop across R is low (most of the voltage drop is across the cell). The resistance of the cell is reduced by light impinging on the cell; its resistance is lowered and the current through the circuit increases causing the voltage drop across the resistor to rise. The voltage across R and the current through the circuit are usually too low to permit substitution of a relay coil for R. However, some photoconductive cells will pass enough current to energize a relay. In most cases, an electronic amplifier is used between the cell load (R) and a relay.

The photovoltaic cell, often called a solar cell, generates a voltage when exposed to light. An example of a photovoltaic cell is shown in Fig. 21. The output power of such a cell is usually so low that an amplifier is required between it and a relay. However,

53

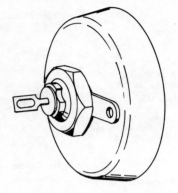

photovoltaic cells can be connected in series, as shown in Fig. 22, to produce sufficient voltage to energize a sensitive relay.

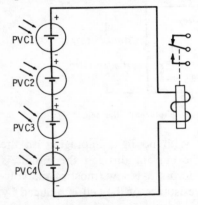

Fig. 22. Circuit employing four photovoltaic cells in series to control a relay.

Courtesy International Rectifier Corp.

The sensitivity of a photovoltaic cell can be increased by forward-biasing it with a DC voltage as shown in Fig. 23. Much of the voltage required to energize the relay is provided by the battery. The rest of the required voltage is furnished by the cell when it intercepts a sufficient amount of light.

The relay connected in series with a photovoltaic cell is necessarily one that requires very low energizing power and whose contacts are very limited in current-carrying capacity. This problem can be overcome by cascading two relays as shown in Fig. 24. In

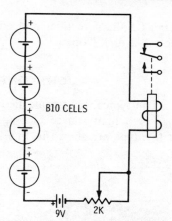

Fig. 23. Photovoltaic cell circuit employing a battery to boost sensitivity.

B10 CELLS

9V   2K

Courtesy International Rectifier Corp.

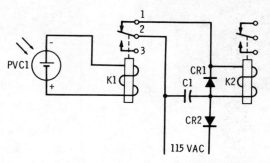

Courtesy International Rectifier Corp.

Fig. 24. Cascaded photovoltaic cell relay circuit.

this circuit, relay *K1* is energized by PVC (photovoltaic cell) or several of them in series (see Fig. 22). When the light energy converted into electrical energy is great enough to normally energize relay *K1*, cutting off the light causes *K1* to drop out and close its NC back contacts (1-2). Relay *K2*, whose contacts will handle more power, is pulled in and its contacts can be used to actuate an alarm. Power for energizing *K2* is obtained from 115-VAC power line through series rectifier *CR2* and relay chatter is eliminated by filter capacitor *C*. Diode *CR1* across the winding of *K2*

55

acts as a shunt rectifier and dampens inductive surges when contacts 1-2 of *K1* open.

LIGHT-CONTROLLED ALARMS

The typical light-controlled alarm or door-control system consists of a light source and a light detector. Typical components of this type are shown in Fig. 25. Light from the unit at the right

Courtesy Veeder-Root

Fig. 25. Light-controlled sensing system. The light source is shown at right.

is focused on the light aperture at the left. If the light beam is prevented from reaching the detector at the left, as when a person passes through the light beam, a relay is tripped and an alarm is sounded—or in the case of a door opener, the door is automatically opened. The light beam may be visible or at invisible infrared frequencies.

When it is impractical to focus the light source at the light detector, the light from the source can be conveyed through fiber optic cables to a lens tube. The light beam is then transmitted through space to a control lens tube, as shown in Fig. 26, which

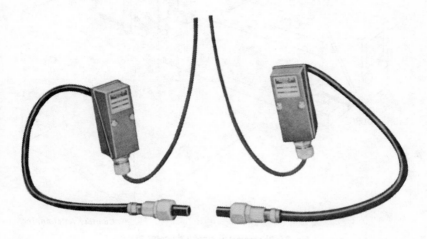

Fig. 26. Light-controlled sensing system utilizing fiber optic remote heads.

intercepts the light and transmits it through a fiber optic cable to the light detector.

The flexible fiber optic cables convey light around corners through crooked paths and even in circles. A fiber optic cable consists of bundles of plastic fibers which convey light.

The light beam system shown in Fig. 27 is used for detecting smoke in an air duct. The light source is focused at the control head. Smoke passing between them is detected by the control head which actuates an alarm.

In lieu of using a separate light source and a separate light detector, they can be combined in a single unit, as shown in Fig. 28. The scanner head has output and input lenses. It transmits a light beam to a mirror-like specular reflective surface which reflects the light back to the detector lens of the scanner head. Any object that blocks passage of light to or from the reflector causes the detector to actuate an alarm.

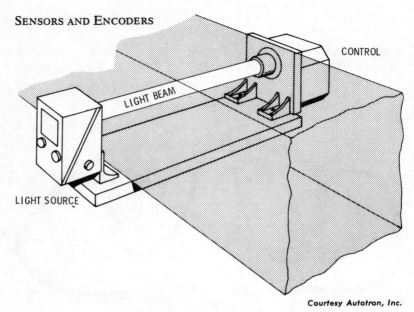

Courtesy Autotron, Inc.

Fig. 27. Photoelectric smoke detector system.

DOTTED LINE REPRESENTS PATH OF REFLECTION - NOT THE LIGHT BEAM

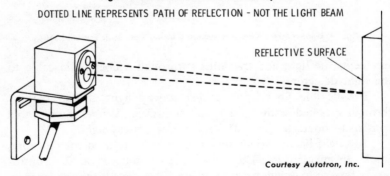

Courtesy Autotron, Inc.

Fig. 28. Photoelectric sensing system utilizing a combination light source and detector head which responds to light reflected from a specular (mirrorlike surface).

A similar system employing a retroreflector is illustrated in Fig. 29. The light beam is projected through a lens to a retroreflective surface which reflects the light back to the detector. The retroreflective surface may be up to 15° from perpendicular with respect to the light beam.

58

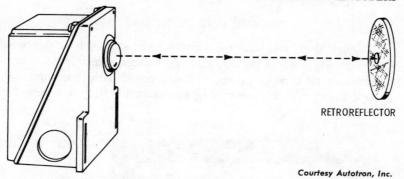

RETROREFLECTOR

Courtesy Autotron, Inc.

Fig. 29. Photoelectric sensing system employing a combination light transmitter which responds to light reflected by a retroreflector.

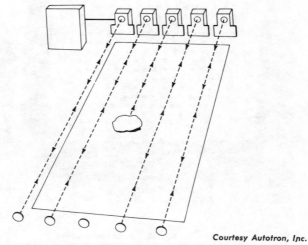

Courtesy Autotron, Inc.

Fig. 30. Example of a large area application of a photoelectric sensing system employing retroreflectors.

An application of this technique is illustrated in Fig. 30. Here, five combination light source/light detector units are used in combination with five retroreflectors. As objects pass through the light beams, the affected detector actuates an alarm. In this illustration, it is shown (as an example) that the middle light beam has been blocked by an object.

59

POWER LINE MONITORS

Failure of electric power can cause an alarm, such as the one shown in Fig. 31, to be actuated. A voltage sensor senses the presence or absence of power. When a power failure occurs, an audible alarm, which is powered by an external battery, is actuated.

Courtesy P.R. Mallory and Co.

Fig. 31. Power line monitor.

A block diagram of a very sensitive power line voltage sensor is shown in Fig. 32. The power line is connected through a filter to an AC-to-DC power supply which provides the power for the rest of the circuitry and to the sensing level potentiometers. After the potentiometers have been set for upper and lower limits, the comparator circuits (each consisting of a summing amplifier, DC amplifier, and trigger circuits) deliver an alarm signal when the line voltage is either too high or too low.

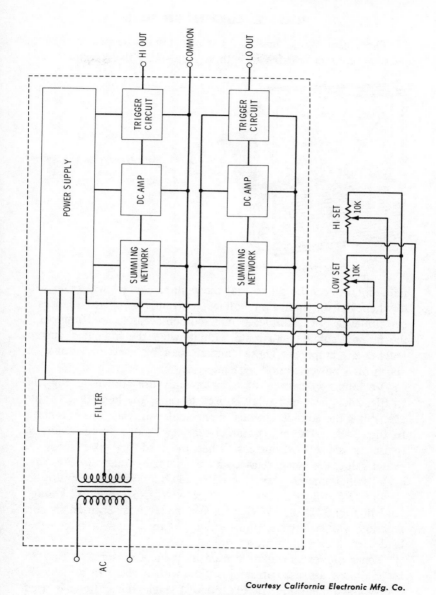

Fig. 32. Block diagram of an AC power line voltage sensor.

VOLTAGE/CURRENT SENSORS

The sensor shown in Fig. 33 is a meter whose pointer has an electrical contact that mates with an adjustable fixed contact. The

Fig. 33. Meter-type voltage or current sensor.

Courtesy Allied Electronics

fixed contact can be set so that the pointer contact will mate with it whenever the indicated voltage, current, or power reaches a certain level. For example, if the fixed contact is set at 10 amperes, the pointer contact will mate with it when the indicated current reaches 10 amperes. These contacts can be used to actuate an alarm or a power shutoff system.

Various applications of a meter-relay are shown in Fig. 34. In Fig. 34A the meter-relay is used to sense the level of DC voltage. When the voltage exceeds the preset level, relay K is energized. In Fig. 34B, a DC milliammeter-relay (with or without shunt R) is used to sense load current. When the load current exceeds the preset value, the meter-relay contacts energize a relay. In Fig. 34C, a DC milliammeter-relay is used in conjunction with a multiplier resistor (R) and diode rectifiers $(CR1\text{-}CR2)$ to sense AC voltage. And in Fig. 34D, an AC load alarm meter-relay is used in conjunction with a current transformer (T) to actuate a relay when load current exceeds a preset value.

Zener diodes can also be used as voltage sensors. In Fig. 35, zener diodes are used in conjunction with a relay to indicate an over-voltage condition. In Fig. 35A, a single zener diode is used.

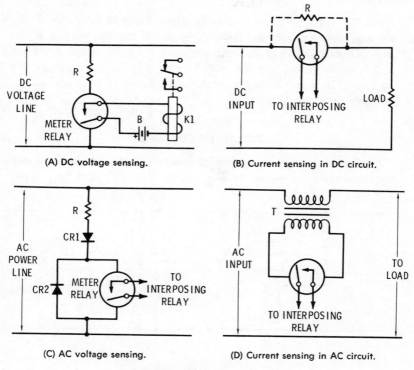

(A) DC voltage sensing.

(B) Current sensing in DC circuit.

(C) AC voltage sensing.

(D) Current sensing in AC circuit.

Fig. 34. Examples of meter-relay applications.

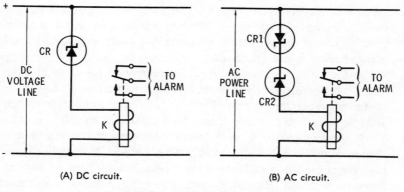

(A) DC circuit.

(B) AC circuit.

Fig. 35. Zener diodes as voltage sensors.

63

If the DC voltage exceeds the avalanche voltage of the zener diode, the relay is energized and lamp *I1* glows. If the DC voltage is too low to cause the zener diode to conduct, the relay is not pulled in and lamp *I2* glows. (An alarm can be used in lieu of either lamp.) In Fig. 35B, a pair of zener diodes are connected back-to-back to perform the same functions.

POLARITY SENSORS

In an alarm system, an off-normal condition can be indicated by a reversal of polarity. In Fig. 36, the use of diodes as polarity

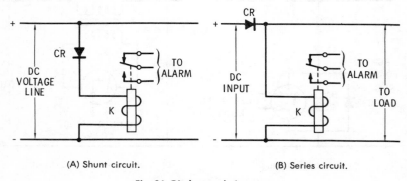

(A) Shunt circuit.   (B) Series circuit.

Fig. 36. Diode as polarity sensor.

sensors is illustrated. In Fig. 36A, relay *K* is energized when the polarity is normal since diode *CR* is forward-biased and acts as an open switch. If the polarity is reversed, the diode is reverse-biased and the relay is not energized.

In Fig. 36B, the diode *(CR)* is in series with the relay and the load. When the polarity is normal, *CR* conducts and relay *K* is energized. When the polarity is reversed, *CR* acts as an open switch and the relay is not energized and load current is cut off.

A device, known as a *Raysistor,* consists of a lamp and a photoconductive cell enclosed in a tiny, plug-in, light-tight chamber. When used in a DC circuit, as shown in Fig. 37A, no current flows through the *Raysistor* lamp when the polarity is normal. When the polarity is reversed, diode *CR* conducts and current

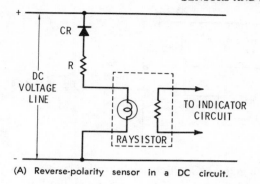

(A) Reverse-polarity sensor in a DC circuit.

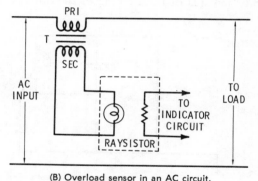

(B) Overload sensor in an AC circuit.

Fig. 37. Raysistors as a sensor.

flows through the *Raysistor* lamp causing a reduction in the resistance of the photoconductive cell.

In Fig. 37B, it is shown how a *Raysistor* can be used as an overload indicator in an AC circuit. As load current through the primary of transformer *T* rises, the voltage across the *Raysistor* lamp also rises, causing a reduction in the resistance of its photoconductive cell, and vice versa.

VEHICLE INTRUSION SENSORS

An automobile theft alarm system is usually actuated by a disturbance to the vehicle's electrical system. The alarm, most often, is the vehicle horn. As shown in Fig. 38, the horn is con-

65

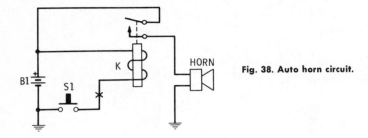

Fig. 38. Auto horn circuit.

trolled by a relay *(K)* which is controlled by the horn button *(S1)* which grounds one side of the winding of the horn relay.

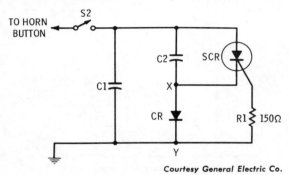

Courtesy General Electric Co.

Fig. 39. Vehicle battery voltage sensor.

The electronic circuit, shown in Fig. 39, employs an SCR and senses the voltage at the ungrounded side of the horn button (point X in Fig. 38). When arm-disarm switch $S2$ (Fig. 39) is closed, capacitor $C1$ is charged to the level of the battery voltage, and $C2$ is charged through diode CR to a fraction of a volt less than $C2$ because of the small voltage drop across CR. After $C2$ has become charged, CR no longer conducts. When any electrical device in the car is turned on (dome light, ignition switch, etc.), there is a small drop in voltage. The charge across $C1$ drops slightly. $C2$ then conducts as it starts to discharge. Point Y becomes positive with respect to X and the SCR is triggered into conduction. The horn circuit is completed through the SCR and diode CR, and the horn continues to sound until $S2$ is opened.

Fig. 40. Automobile burglar alarm
control unit.

Courtesy Metra Electronics Corp.

An example of a commercially available automotive burglar
alarm tripper is shown in Fig. 40. Another type of automotive

Courtesy Barney Ephraim

Fig. 41. Inductive auto burglar alarm control.

burglar alarm tripper is shown in Fig. 41. It is attached to the un-grounded battery cable and operates on the inductive kick principle. As illustrated in Fig. 42, the battery cable is inductively

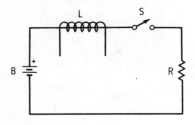

Fig. 42. Inductive-kick demonstration circuit.

coupled to a winding within the box. A surge of current through the cable causes a momentary voltage to be developed across the coil which is used to trigger an electronic switch.

WATER SENSORS

A sensor which detects surface water is shown in Fig. 43. When moist, it develops an output signal which can be used to

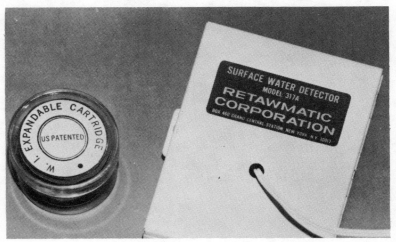

Courtesy Retawmatic Corp.

Fig. 43. A water detector.

trigger an alarm. The sensor shown in Fig. 44 senses the presence of water in oil.

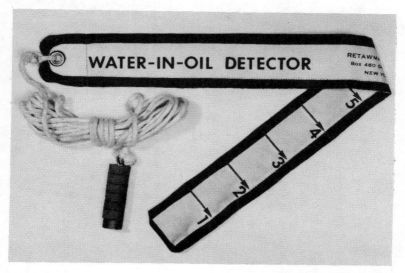

Fig. 44. A water-in-oil detector.

ULTRASONIC SENSORS

An ultrasonic sensor generates and radiates sound waves which are inaudible to the human ear. These waves permeate a room. When an object in the room moves (such as a human being), these waves are disturbed and reflected; these changes are sensed and used to activate an alarm. An example of an ultrasonic movement detector is shown in Fig. 45. It contains both the detector and an audible alarm.

INFRARED SENSORS

The presence of human beings can be detected by sensors that are responsive to radiated infrared energy. Infrared radiation is similar to visible light but has a longer wave length—too long to

Courtesy P.R. Mallory and Co.

Fig. 45. Ultrasonic movement sensor.

be seen by the eye. Infrared waves are emitted by many common objects such as radiators, electric heaters, stoves, incandescent lamps, animals, and human beings. A live human body generates heat and, as a result, emits infrared energy.

Infrared radiation can be detected with a sensor employing a small piece (chip) of triglycine sulphate (TGS) against which electrodes are placed. (See Fig. 46.) When infrared radiation is sensed by the TGS chip, it operates as a bolometer (a device whose resistance changes with temperature). The detector assembly consists of a metal tube with a window at one end behind which the chip is mounted. The detector assembly is mounted in a plastic pipe behind an optical lens. The incident radiation is gathered and focused by the lens which also limits the field of view. By making the field of view narrow, a person passing through this field will cause the production of a stronger analog signal. Such a

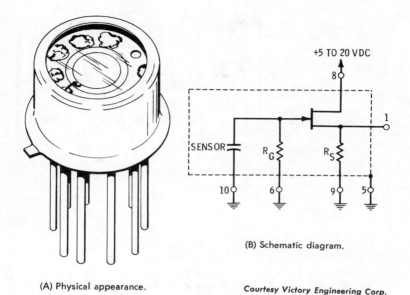

(B) Schematic diagram.

(A) Physical appearance.

Courtesy Victory Engineering Corp.

Fig. 46. Example of an infrared detector.

sensor detects the presence of a person whose infrared radiation is stronger than that of slightly cooler objects in the background.

The output of the detector is fed to an electronic amplifier system which drives a relay. Since an infrared sensor can sense the heat emitted by a radiator, it should be focused at a surface which is thermally stable. The advantage of an infrared sensor is that only a receiver is required since the transmitter is a human being or other warm object.

RADAR SENSORS

A so-called radar sensor radiates microwaves—radio waves whose frequency is above 900 MHz. In a conventional radar system used for detection of distant object, microwave pulses (short bursts of RF energy) are transmitted outward by a directional antenna, as shown in Fig. 47. When a pulse strikes a solid object, it is reflected back to the antenna. The time required for a pulse

71

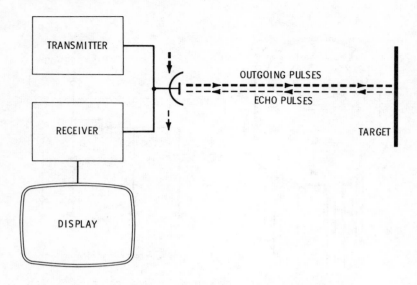

Fig. 47. Radar distance measuring principle.

to reach the target and return to its source is measured by an electronic system employing a cathode-ray tube (somewhat like a TV picture tube) calibrated in miles or kilometers.

A radar vehicle detector transmits microwave energy downward toward the street, as shown in Fig. 48. When a vehicle passes

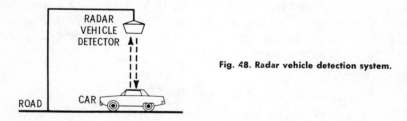

Fig. 48. Radar vehicle detection system.

under the detector, the length of the round-trip microwave path is shortened because the microwave energy is reflected back to the source by the vehicle. When this happens, a relay within the detector is actuated. Operation of the relay by a passing vehicle can be used to actuate an alarm when such a system is used to detect unauthorized movement of vehicles from a parking lot or building. When installed over public roads, radar vehicle sensors are used to trigger traffic signal controllers and/or to count the number of vehicles passing a given location.

Radar intrusion detectors, examples of which are shown in Fig. 49 and Fig. 50, also radiate microwave energy which travels

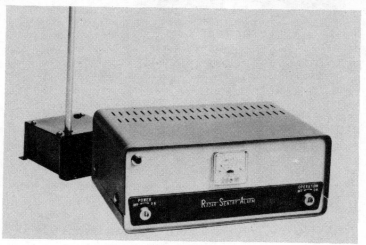

Fig. 49. Radar sentry alarm system.

to the walls of the protected room. When an intruder enters the room, the microwave field is disturbed. This is sensed by the microwave transceiver and an alarm is actuated.

A radar system may detect a change in the round-trip signal travel distance or it may also detect the speed at which the travel distance change occurs. The latter technique employs the *Doppler effect*. The pitch of a sound or, in the case of a *Doppler* radar system, the frequency of the returned microwave energy, is varied.

Radar systems are widely used on land for observing the movements of aircraft above the ground, on board aircraft for observing clouds and air turbulence, and on ships for observing other vessels and the shore line. In addition, radar is used for observing the movements of vehicles on the ground. At John F. Kennedy Airport

Fig. 50. Radar intrusion detector.

in New York, for example, a radar system scans the airport area and its viewing screen displays the location and direction of travel of aircraft and other vehicles on the ground. A similar system could be used in a large industrial complex, or in a railroad yard, to observe the movements of vehicles on the ground.

As previously shown in Fig. 47, the radar antenna emits microwave pulses which are reflected by targets back to the radar antenna. The antenna rotates through a continuous circle so that the pulses strike one target after the other. What is "seen" by the antenna is "painted" on the radar viewing screen which is calibrated in terms of both distance and azimuth.

MAGNETOMETERS

A magnetometer is a device that senses and can be used to measure the earth's magnetism and to sense disturbances to the earth's magnetic field. During World War II, an airborne system employing the magnetometer was developed for the purpose of detecting submerged submarines. The system sensed disturbances to the earth's magnetic field caused by the presence of a submarine.

In security applications, magnetometers are used in weapons detectors and as movement sensors. The *Tempter MK-2* intruder alarm (made by *Infinetics, Inc.)* is a small rectangular unit (5" x 6" x 1.5") which contains a magnetometer, an audible alarm, the

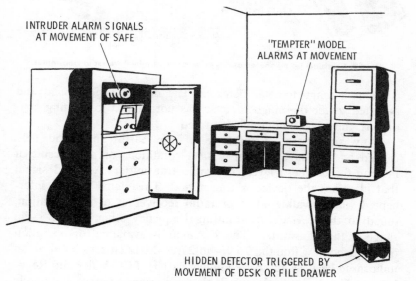

INTRUDER ALARM SIGNALS
AT MOVEMENT OF SAFE

"TEMPTER" MODEL
ALARMS AT MOVEMENT

HIDDEN DETECTOR TRIGGERED BY
MOVEMENT OF DESK OR FILE DRAWER

Fig. 51. Application of a magnetometer-type sensor.

required electronic circuitry, and batteries. Fig. 51 shows three applications of the device. Once placed in position, the device automatically zeroes itself to its surroundings within a few moments. Subsequent movement of either the unit itself or the safe door, desk, file drawers, or metal waste basket will trigger the device, which will sound an audio alarm that cannot be silenced for 1½ minutes.

The same company manufactures a portable radio transmitter, known as the *Tattletale,* whose walkie-talkie type housing (Fig. 52)

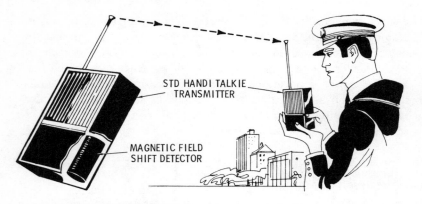

STD HANDI TALKIE
TRANSMITTER

MAGNETIC FIELD
SHIFT DETECTOR

Fig. 52. Combination magnetometer-type sensor and miniature radio transmitter.

contains a magnetometer detector. The device is positioned and adjusted. After the magnetometer has normalized to existing conditions, the triggering circuit is armed.

Any subsequent disturbance of the earth's magnetic field caused by a change in nearby steel conditions or as a result of moving the device, triggers the radio transmitter. A coded signal that identifies the device is transmitted. This signal can be intercepted with a walkie-talkie or radio receiver at a fixed location, tuned to the device's transmitting frequency when within radio range of the transmitter. The *Tattletale* is available for operation on frequencies within the 26.96- to 27.26-MHz citizens band on an unlicensed basis as authorized under Part 15 FCC Rules and Regulations. The device is also available for operation on specific public safety and industrial radio channels under an FCC radio station license.

WALK-THROUGH WEAPONS DETECTORS

Walk-through metal detectors, used at airports and other portals, are of the "active" or "passive" type. The *Sperry Rand* SMD-1000 weapons detector, shown in Fig. 53, employs the "active-element" balanced-field principle and detects both ferrous and nonferrous metals. As can be seen in the illustration, the SMD-

Fig. 53. Active-type weapons detector.

1000 consists of two assemblies, a walk-through gate and a control console which can be pedestal-mounted (as shown) or placed on a desk counter top or bracket-mounted to a wall.

The detecting elements are molded into the vertical columns of the fiberglas walk-through gate. The electronic circuits are on printed-circuit boards contained within the control console. The gate and control console are interconnected through a 15-foot cable.

The AC-powered (115-230 VAC) control console has six push buttons and four control knobs balance and sensitivity adjustments and mode selection. Indicators include a meter, an out-of-balance light, a right side metal-presence light, a left side metal-presence light and an audible alarm whose use is optional.

Courtesy Infinetics, Inc.

Fig. 54. Passive-type weapons detector.

The *Friskem* types 1 and 2 walk-through weapons detectors employ two pipe-like detector towers, as shown in Fig. 54. Each of the six-foot high aluminum towers contains two ferrous-metal detectors which are connected to a monitor unit through plug-in cables. This system employs "passive" magnetometer principle which senses disturbances to the earth's magnetic field.

The monitor unit has operating control knobs, a meter and an alarm light. Electric power for operation of the system may be AC at 90-250 volts, 45-420 Hz, or eight mercury cells which are installed within the monitor unit housing.

A remote alarm light unit, a remote audio alarm unit, or a remote audio and light alarm unit can be plug-connected to the monitor unit through a 50-foot cable. When any of the remote alarm units are connected to the system, the alarm light on the front panel of the monitor unit is disconnected.

The ½-inch blue remote alarm light is contained in a 2-inch wooden cube. The remote audio alarm contains an audio horn within a 2-inch square aluminum box. The combination remote audio and light alarm components are contained within a 2-inch by 4-inch aluminum box which has a switch for selecting either or both the light or horn plus a horn volume control.

The light and/or horn are controlled by a relay in the monitor unit. The relay contacts have a rated capacity of 10 amperes but the manufacturer recommends that the load current not exceed 5 amperes.

The alarm output voltage is normally only momentary. However, holding contacts can be provided when required. A release button is used to release the holding contacts.

In addition to the type of detector tower installation shown previously in Fig. 54, optional detector installations are illustrated in Fig. 55. The detectors may be installed on the hidden side of the wall of an entrance or exit, as shown in Fig. 55A, where they won't be seen by the person being checked. The detectors can be concealed in signholders as shown in Fig. 55B, or in fence posts as shown in Fig. 5C. Or, the detector tower can be used as a floor-rack as shown in Fig. 55D, or as a signpost attached to an ashtray as shown in Fig.55E. Or, the detector tower can be used as a floor-

SENSORS AND ENCODERS

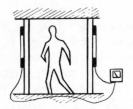

A DETECTORS MAY BE ON HIDDEN SIDE OF WALL
(AS WELL AS PASSAGE SIDE).
SUSPECT DOES NOT REALIZE EXAMINATION.

B DETECTORS CONCEALED IN SIGNHOLDER.
NOTE THEY ARE SPACED FROM DESK
TO EASE SCREENING OF SUSPECTS BODY.

C
GUIDE FENCE SEPARATES SUSPECTS AND PREVENTS REMINGLING.
DETECTORS HIDDEN AS FENCE POSTS OR SIGNHOLDERS.
NOTE THAT HIGH DESK ELIMINATES LUNCH BOX FROM
CONSIDERATION AND ONLY SUSPECTS BODY IS EXAMINED.

D DETECTOR TOWER
DISGUISED AS HAT RACK.

E DETECTOR TOWER
DISGUISED AS
SIGN POST ON ASH TRAY

F DETECTOR TOWER AS
FLOOR-TO-CEILING POLE.
SCREW-JACK BASE ALLOWS
ADJUSTMENT RANGE FOR PORTABILITY.
GOOD METHOD OF STURDY MOUNTING
WHERE SOLID SUPPORTS NOT AVAILABLE

G DETECTOR TOWER
DISGUIDED AS
"PLANTER" SUPPORT

Fig. 55. Optional weapons detector installations.

to-ceiling pole, secured by a screw-jack base as shown in Fig. 55F. Still another alternative is to use the detector tower as a plant support, as shown in Fig. 55G.

These towers can provide concentrated search capability, as shown in Fig. 56A, when two detectors are contained in each tower, or augmented search capability, as shown in Fig. 56B, when four detectors are contained in each tower.

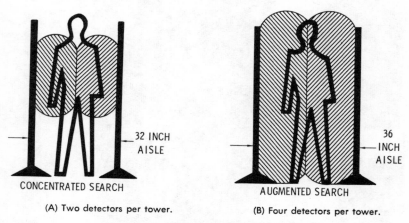

32 INCH
AISLE

36
INCH
AISLE

CONCENTRATED SEARCH

AUGMENTED SEARCH

(A) Two detectors per tower.

(B) Four detectors per tower.

Fig. 56. Concentrated-search weapons detectors.

The *Friskem* type-3 walk-through weapons detector system, shown in Fig. 57, employs four detectors in each tower. In addition to a monitor unit, a viewer is provided which shows the location of a weapon on a person's body.

MOBILE WEAPONS DETECTORS

A weapons detector can be built into a nightstick or flashlight to enable search of a person without personal contact, as illustrated in Fig. 58. Both the *Friskem* nightstick and the *Friskem* flashlight sense disturbances in the earth's magnetic field caused by the presence of iron or steel, and are sensitive enough to detect knives, razor blades, hat pins, sharpened tools, as well as guns, through the heaviest clothing. The devices, as shown in Fig. 58,

81

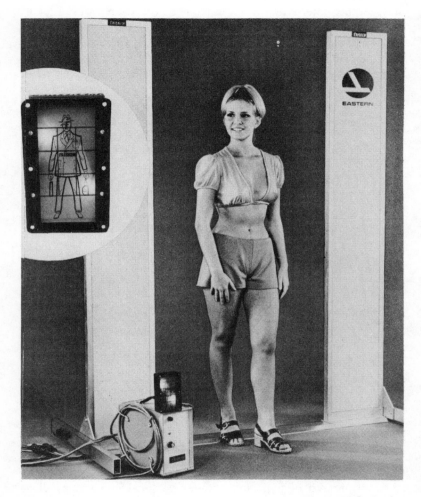

Courtesy Infinetics, Inc.

Fig. 57. Weapons-detector system with weapon-location viewer.

have range and meter zero control knobs and a meter indicator, and operate from self-contained batteries.

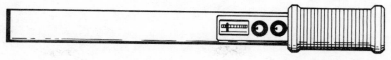

Courtesy Infinetics, Inc.

Fig. 58. Handheld-weapons detector.

The *Friskem Bodyguard* search detector system is worn by a person and is concealed by clothing. A magnetic detector cartridge is strapped to the forearm and is connected through wires to a waistbelt control module. The user circulates through a crowd, unobtrusively moving the arm to which the detector is attached. Upon sensing a firearm or other ferrous object, the user receives a silent signal directly to the body.

WEAPONS DETECTOR SITES

The passive, magnetometer type of walk-through weapons detector will work better if its site is carefully selected. Site selection can be simplified by using a magnetic field strength survey instrument, (FSI), such as the *Friskem MK-1*. The procedures are as follows:

1. Find north (see Fig. 59A) by holding the FSI horizontally out in space and free from close-by steel, rotating the instrument through a 360-degree compass orientation to obtain the highest meter indication. The long dimension of the instrument case, toward the inclinometer, now points toward magnetic North.

2. Without changing the north orientation, level the FSI so the ball is centered on zero degrees (see Fig. 59A). The meter now indicates the horizontal vector of the total magnetic field.

3. Again, without changing the north orientation, tilt the FSI vertically until the ball is on 90 degrees (see Fig. 59B). The meter now indicates the vertical vector of the total magnetic field.

4. Without changing the north orientation, tilt the FSI between horizontal and vertical to obtain the highest meter reading

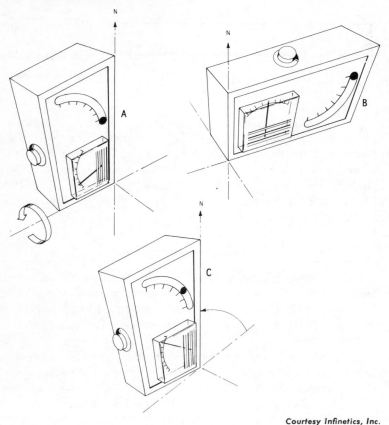

Fig. 59. Use of magnetic field strength survey instrument for selection of sites for a magnetometer-type weapon detector.

(see Fig. 59C). This is the total magnetic field; the inclinometer ball will directly indicate the angle of inclination.

The best magnetic detector site is:

(a) Where the magnetic field is not distorted by visible items like steel beams and walls, or invisible fields from power cables, motors, etc.

(b) Where the magnetic field is the maximum available value.

    (c) Where the persons to be checked walk in a north-south rather than east-west direction. (Not essential, but better.)

As a rule of thumb, try not to locate a magnetic detector where:

    (a) The magnetic field is less than 80 percent of normal for a geographical area.

    (b) The plane of space which contains the person being examined and the detector towers varies more than 20 percent overall in magnetic value.

If the ambient magnetic field strength is below desirable levels, equipment modifications may be made. For example, some walk-through detectors can be supplied with increased detection potential for its precalibrated sensitivity positions.

Surveying Detector Sites

Absolute Readings: Record a few careful readings in optimum areas to establish a normal standard for the building or area of interest. This will allow a cross reference to charts of the magnetic fields to be expected of the specific geographic area and charts of confidence levels for selected search thresholds. See Figs. 60, 61, 62, and 63.

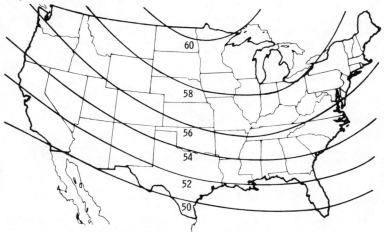

Fig. 60. Isodynamic plot of total magnetic field intensity in kilogammas.

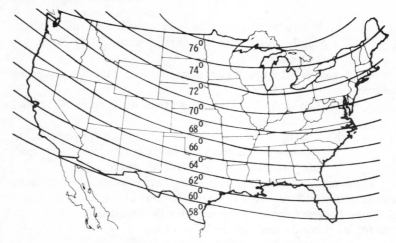

Fig. 61. Isoclinic plot of magnetic inclination in degrees.

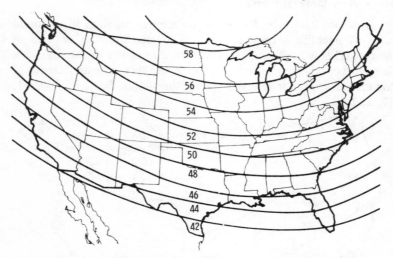

Fig. 62. Isodynamic plot of vertical field intensity in kilogammas.

FAST SURVEY CHECKS

Hold the FSI roughly vertically and note the initial meter reading. Starting about 6 feet above the ground, sweep horizontally

86

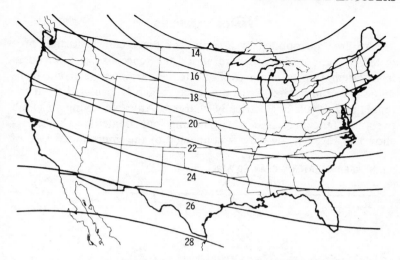

Fig. 63. Isodynamic plot of horizontal field intensity in kilogammas.

back and forth across the approximate 5-foot span where it is intended to place the detector. Lower each sweep about 12 inches and finish about 8 inches above the ground. The site is satisfactorily free of distortion if the meter readings do not vary more than 20 percent overall. The actual reading is a rough approximation of the vertical field and may be compared to that absolute. Be highly suspicious of any areas in the continental U.S. where the vertical readings are not at least 35 kilogammas.

LOOP DETECTORS

Loop detectors, buried below the surface of the ground, are used for sensing the presence of a vehicle, such as an auto, truck, or railroad car. Some are also connected to electronic devices which also indicate whether the detected vehicle is standing or in motion. The loop detector itself is a wire which senses a change in the magnetic field within its sensing range. In security applications, loop detectors can be used for sensing the movement of vehicles in a driveway and the presence or absence of vehicles in a parking lot or at a loading platform.

87

FENCE SENSORS

An area surrounded by a chain-link fence can be further protected by running barbed wire above the fence to deter intruders from attempting to climb over the fence. Another deterrent technique is to run a wire above the fence, which is insulated from the fence, and which is electrically charged. Any one trying to climb over the fence receives a frightening but nonlethal shock. As shown in Fig. 64, the wire is connected to the ungrounded side of

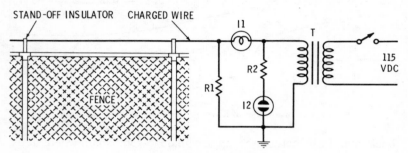

Fig. 64. Fence protection circuit.

the 115-volt AC power line through a low-wattage lamp. Since the fence itself is grounded, any one touching both the fence and the wire will receive an electrical shock. Accidental shorting of the wire to the fence will cause the lamp to light. Normally, extremely low current (about 0.001 ampere) flows through the circuit —just enough to keep neon lamp *I2* glowing to indicate that the deterrent wire is hot with respect to ground.

The same technique has been used to keep dogs away from garbage cans. An electrical engineer whose garbage cans were frequently knocked down by stray dogs, placed the cans on bricks to insulate them from the ground. Each can was connected to the ungrounded side of the 115 VAC power line through a flexible wire, terminated in an alligator clip for easy connection, and a low-wattage lamp. Once the dogs touched the cans, the shock taught them a lesson and they never returned. Extreme care should be exercised when this technique is used with a fence or other objects to limit the current so as to prevent lethal shock. The series lamp should have a rating of 7.5 watts or less (at 115 VAC). In lieu of a lamp, a 27,000-ohm resistor or 0.1-MF capacitor can be used which will limit current to less than 0.005 ampere.

A safer fence sensor consists of parallel wire above and insulated from a metal fence, as shown in Fig. 65, which in combina-

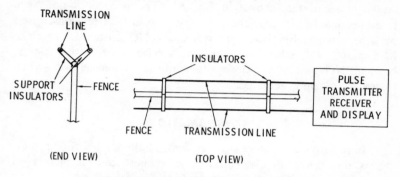

Fig. 65. High-frequeny pulse sensing system for fences.

tion with the fence forms an open-wire transmission line. If the wire and the fence are evenly spaced, the transmission line will have a uniform characteristic impedance. If the wire is touched or is in close proximity to a person attempting to scale the fence, the characteristic impedance of the transmission line is changed at that point. This change in impedance can be detected with an electronic system, similar to those used for testing telephone cables and other transmission lines, which applies high-frequency pulses

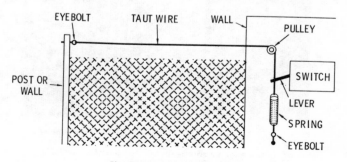

Fig. 66. Taut-wire fence alarm.

89

to the transmission line and which utilizes an oscilloscope to observe any change in the time of pulses returning as echoes.

This type of sensing system must be carefully engineered and requires monitoring with an oscilloscope. Its primary applications are at prisons and high-security areas. Much simpler is to use the taut-wire technique, shown in Fig. 66. The wire does not have to be insulated from the fence. An increase in wire tension caused by a person grabbing the wire will cause NO switch *S1* to close its contacts. Or, when wire tension is relaxed or if the wire is broken, NO switch *S2* closes its contacts. When either switch closes, the alarm is actuated.

SENSORMATIC

Many large department stores and small neighborhood merchants now have an electronic "big brother" aid in their fight

Courtesy Sensormatic Electronics Corp.

**Fig. 67. Sensormatic security tag which triggers the electronic
device when placed in the magnetic field of the sensor.**

against shoplifters who annually steal millions of dollars in merchandise. This electronic device is called *Sensormatic*. A tag, shown in Fig. 67, is attached to the garment which will trigger the electronic device if it is passed through this magnetic field.

This electronic system is also used in many major manufacturing corporations as a protection against portable hand tool theft with the use of a security collar as shown in Fig. 68. Another

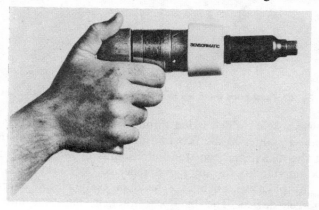

Courtesy Sensormatic Electronics Corp.

Fig. 68. A Sensormatic security collar attached to a portable hand tool.

way of attaching this security device on hand tools is by means of pistol grips which are permanently bonded to the tool handle as shown in Fig. 69.

Operation of System

The 120 volt, 60 Hz/220 volt, 50 Hz power input is connected to the input power transformers which drop this voltage to 40 volts at 50/60 Hz. The 40 volts is fed to the power supply as shown in the block diagram in Fig. 70. The power supply consists basically of a −16 volt regulator and a +16 volt regulator to drive the various circuits. The 24 volts AC is used to drive the alarm circuits.

The transmitter, nominally at 915 MHz, is powered by the −16 volts output from the power supply. This generates the

Courtesy Sensormatic Electronics Corp.

Fig. 69. Pistol grips which are permanently attached to the tool handle.

microwave signal which is fed through an isolator, bandpass filter and power splitter to the two transmit antennas. The isolator preserves the match between transmitters thus maintaining frequency and power stability for any power reflected back into the antennas from any blockage, such as a hand or body placed in front of the trigger device. The bandpass filter in the transmitter arm serves to prevent off-frequency signals from being transmitted and interfering with other systems. The power divider splits the transmitter signal and directs the energy to two antennas, located one on each side of the aperture being protected.

The aperture being protected is thus filled with a microwave signal at the transmitter frequency. The aperture is also illuminated by an electrostatic field. This field is produced by applying a 50 kHz sine-wave voltage from a generator (described later) to two metallic plates, one in each pedestal on either side of the aperture. Actually the 50 kHz signal is varied around 50 kHz as will be described later. It is called 50 kHz for convenience. Pedestal installations are shown in Fig. 71.

When a tag enters the combined fields, at a point where both fields are of sufficient strength, the nonlinear characteristics of the semiconductor on the tag act to produce a mixing or combining action whereby the two signals are either added or subtracted. The resultant composite signal is then reradiated by the

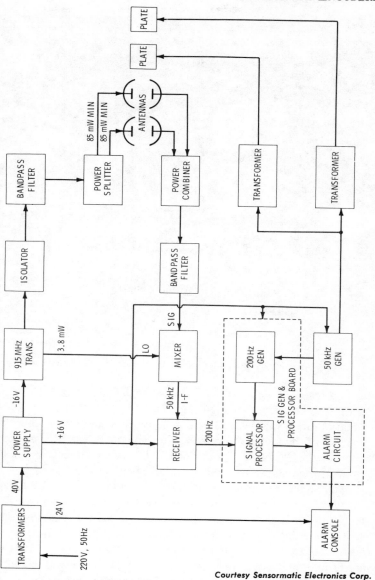

Courtesy Sensormatic Electronics Corp.

Fig. 70. Block diagram of the Sensormatic electronic device.

93

Courtesy Sensormatic Electronics Corp.

Fig. 71. Triggering devices (called pedestals) installed in a retail clothing store.

tag and received by the system. Note that the mixing process occurs as a threshold effect. Mixing occurs strongly at a very sharp line of demarkation in the fields. There is no weak signal effect where the presence of the tag is qustionable. Further, the mixing line or alarm range of the system is controllable by varying either the voltage applied to the plates, transmitter power level, or both.

Any signal generated by a tag in the aperture, on the receive side of the system, is picked up by the receive antennas. The signals in each antenna are added in the power combiner and passed into the receive bandpass filter. This filter is tuned to the transmitter frequency and thus prevents out-of-hand signals from interfering or "capturing" the receiver. The received signal is then fed into the mixer where it is beat against a low level (approximately 5 mw) transmitter sample. The received signal and transmitter signal are "mixed" in the mixer diode and the 50 kHz difference between the two is demodulated and passed out of the mixer output. In essence, the 50 kHz signal combined with the transmitter microwave signal by the tag in the aperture is removed from the microwave signal by the reverse process in the mixer and it is this 50 kHz that is processed to produce an alarm.

The 50 kHz output of the mixer enters the receiver and is filtered to remove any extraneous modulation products that may have been imposed on the tag in the aperture of the system. It is then amplified and fed into a limiter-amplifier.

The 50 kHz modulation frequency is not actually a single frequency sine wave as mentioned above, but rather a variable frequency. Thus, a 50 kHz carrier is not 50 kHz, but is 49 kHz and 51 kHz with the frequency changing (deviating) at a 100 Hz to 500 Hz rate. Typically the carrier is varied at approximately 200 Hz, but other values are used depending upon installation requirements.

The limiter-amplifier also contains a detector which further demodulates the signal and extracts the deviation that was additionally imposed on the 50 kHz voltage signal. An oscillator generates a 200 Hz square wave which is applied to the 50 kHz oscillator as an external modulation, as well as being used as a reference comparison signal in the alarm logic circuitry.

A 50 kHz square wave is generated in an oscillator and, with the application of the 200 Hz external modulation, deviates between 49 kHz and 51 kHz. The square wave is then filtered to produce a sine wave. The 50 kHz is conducted by coaxial cables to reach a 20:1 step-up transformer in each pedestal to achieve the necessary electrostatic field intensity. For a typical installation this is approximately 400 volts peak-to-peak on each plate.

The alarm logic circuitry compares the received 200 Hz signal with the 200 Hz reference signal that was applied to the 50 kHz electrostatic field voltage. It also compares the two for phase coherence. It then counts a specified number (typically 8 or 12) of distortion-free pulses to verify that the received signal is being generated by a tag rather than being a randomly generated signal. The counter output activates the alarm circuits which activates both a one-shot alarm, as well as an oscillating alarm, either one or both of which may be connected at the customer's option.

Thus, to produce an alarm, four (4) rather stringent conditions must be satisfied:

1. The received microwave signal must differ from the transmitted frequency by 50 kHz or whatever value the frequency is set. Unless this difference exists it will not pass through the receiver input filter for further processing.

2. The 50 kHz (nominal) frequency must deviate between the 49 kHz and 51 kHz frequencies at the proper 100 Hz to 500 Hz rate.

3. The 100-500 Hz deviation signal must agree within narrow phase limits with the 100-500 Hz reference signal.

4. The received signal having all the above characteristics must be distortion-free for a predetermined number of pulses.

The requirement upon the received signal of having to meet the above four conditions simultaneously insures to an extremely high probability that any alarm is produced by a tag rather than a spurious signal.

Area Surveillance

Another type of security system gaining in popularity is *CompuVision,* a product of *Sensormatic Electronics.* See Fig. 72. *CompuVision* is a unique marriage of digital computer and CCTV technologies, applied to the field of industrial, commercial, mercantile, government and professonal security. Also, see Chapter 8. The system allows one man to effectively monitor many locations, freeing security personnel to other important jobs.

Each *CompuVision* installed is specifically tailored to the customer's requirements, yet many of its components and accessories are standard shelf items. It's virtually foolproof and invulnerable to jamming or human error. Operation is effective even though an intruder has full knowledge of its existence and location.

This system can be used effectively in underground parking garages as well as warehouses, offices, laboratories, manufacturing plants, retail stores and as an automatic fire and smoke detector.

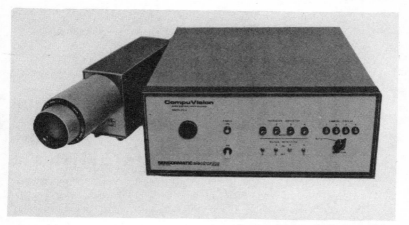

Courtesy Sensormatic Electronics Corp.

Fig. 72. CompuVision area surveillance system.

The heart of the system is the main motion detector; essentially a digital computer that absorbs information transmitted by the CCTV cameras. Normally the television monitor screens linked to the system remain blank. Then, the instant movement is detected in one of the critical areas, the scene under surveillance is displayed on the screen. An audible alarm is sounded, and a light on the control panel comes on, indicating specific location being threatened.

This is only one phase of the CCTV system but with a little imagination there is no limit to the useful purpose it can serve.

97

CHAPTER 4

Indicators and Alarms

An "indicator" may be a lamp, annunciator, or other silent device which displays a yes-or-no status indication or quantitative information. An "alarm", on the other hand, may be a bell, horn, or siren which attracts attention by the sound it produces, or it may be a flashing beacon lamp or other visual attention-attracting device.

COUNTERS

In a security system, it may be important to know how many persons or vehicles enter or leave a protected area. The output of a sensor can be fed directly (or through interposing electronic equipment) to an electromechanical counter, such as the one shown in Fig. 1. Every time an open-or-close sensor is actuated, it increases the displayed number by 1.

When an alarm should be actuated when more than a predetermined number of events take place, a predetermining counter, such as the one shown in Fig. 2, can be utilized. It can be preset to a specific number which is displayed at the right. When the actual count exceeds the predetermined number, an alarm is actuated or access gates or doors are automatically locked.

Counters of this type are actuated by a DC voltage applied through an NO switch or relay contacts or by an NC switch through an interposing relay.

Courtesy Veeder-Root

Fig. 1. An event counter.

Courtesy Veeder-Root

Fig. 2. An event counter with preset maximum count.

ACOUSTIC ALARMS

The most common types of acoustic alarms are electrically-energized bells and buzzers, examples of which are shown in Fig. 3 and Fig. 4. Most bells will operate with either AC or DC applied

99

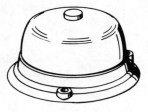

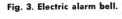
Fig. 3. Electric alarm bell.

Courtesy Radio Shack

Fig. 4. Electric alarm buzzer.

Courtesy Radio Shack

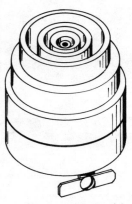

Fig. 5. Sonalert warning device.

Courtesy P.R. Mallory and Co.

if they have NC contacts driven by the armature. Bells and buzzers designed for AC operation only do not require such contacts if their response time is quick enough to follow the polarity reversals of the AC supply voltage.

An example of a sophisticated acoustic alarm is shown in Fig. 5. Although very small physically, these alarm devices generate high sound levels. Various models are available which are operable from DC or AC voltages and which generate continuous-tone or warbling sounds. Another example of a compact electronic acoustic alarm is the *Buzztone* shown in Fig. 6.

Courtesy C.A. Briggs Co., Inc.

Fig. 6. Highly audible electronic buzzer.

An automobile-type horn, designed for operation from a 6- or 12-volt DC source, is also an effective acoustic alarm. An example of a horn-type acoustic alarm, device is illustrated in Fig. 7. This particular alarm device contains a twin *Klaxon* horn

Fig. 7. Twin-Klaxon horn alarm.

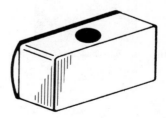

Courtesy Electronic Instrument Co., Inc.

inside an attractive housing and which is operable from a 6-volt DC source.

101

Sirens are also widely used as acoustic alarms. They are available with 6- or 12- volt DC or 115-volt AC drive motors. In addition to motor-driven sirens, electronic sirens are available. The siren-sound is generated electronically amplified and fed to a speaker. Fig. 8 shows a compact siren-sound generator/amplifier and the speaker used to project the sound.

Courtesy Teletronics, Inc.

Fig. 8. Electronic siren and speaker.

VISUAL ALARMS

When a security alarm system is triggered, the alarm may be acoustic or visual or both. A rotating and/or flashing beacon lamp, such as the type used on emergency vehicles, can be an effective attention-getter. They are available in both DC- and AC-operated types.

Fig. 9. Electronic strobe light alarm.

Courtesy Electronic Instrument Co., Inc.

Unique as an attention getter is an electronic strobe light, such as the one shown in Fig. 9. The bright flashes of light can startle an intruder and call the attention of others to the nonexpected sensation. Strobe lights are available for 6- or 12-volt DC or 115-volt AC operation.

LAMP INDICATORS

The incandescent lamp is the most commonly used type of status indicator. They are available in a large variety of voltage, current, and candlepower ratings, in various shapes and with

Table 1. Incandescent Lamps

Mfr's Type	Volts	Amps	Base	Bulb Style	Mfr's Type	Volts	Amps	Base	Bulb Style
PR-2	2.4	.50	S.C. F	B-3½	405	6.5	.50	Screw	G-4½
PR-3	3.6	.50	S.C. F.	B-3½	406	2.6	.30	Screw	G-4½
PR-4	2.3	.27	S.C. F.	B-3½	407	4.9	.30	Screw	G-4½
PR-6	2.47	.30	S.C. F.	B-3½	425	5	.50	Screw	G-4½
PR-12	5.95	.50	S.C. F.	B-3½	432	18.0	.25	Screw	G-4½
PR-13	4.75	.50	S.C. F.	B-3½	433	18	.25	Bayonet	G-4½
6	6.4	3.0	D.C. Bayonet	S-8	509K	24	.18	Cand. Screw	G-6
12	6.3	.15	Min. 2-pin	G-3½	680	5	.060	Wire Term.	T-1
13	3.7	.30	Screw	G-3½	682	5	.060	Sub-Mid. F.	T-1
14	2.5	.30	Screw	G-3½	683	5	.060	Wire Term.	T-1
24E	24	.035	Tel. Slide	T-2	685	5	.060	Sub-Mid. F.	T-1
24X	24	.035	Tel. Slide	T-2	715	5	.115	Wire Term.	T-1
39	6.3	.36	Bayonet	T-3¼	755	6.3	.15	Min. Bay.	T-3¼
40	6.8	.15	Screw	T-3¼	756	14	.08	Min. Bay.	T-3¼
41	2.5	.50	Screw	T-3¼	757	28	.08	Bayonet	T-3¼
43	2.5	.50	Bayonet	T-3¼	CM8-713	5.0	.075	Wire Term.	T-1
44	6.3	.25	Bayonet	T-3¼	CM8-714	5.0	.075	Sub-Mid. F.	T-1
45	3.2	.35	Bayonet	T-3¼	370	18	.04	S.C. Midget	T-1¾
46	6.3	.25	Screw	T-3¼	375	3	.015	S.C. Mid. F.	T-1¾
47	6.3	.15	Bayonet	T-3¼	380	6.3	.04	Mid. Flanged	T-1¾
48	2.0	.06	Screw	T-3¼	381	6.3	.20	Mid. Flanged	T-1¾
48C	48	.035	Tel. Slide	T-2	382	14	.08	Mid. Flanged	T-1¾
49	2.0	.06	Bayonet	T-3¼	386	14	.08	Mid. Grooved	T-1¾
50	7.5	1 c.p.	Screw	G-3½	387	28	.04	Mid. Flanged	T-1¾
51	7.5	1 c.p.	Bayonet	G-3½	388	28	.04	Mid. Grooved	T-1¾
52	14.4	.10	Screw	G-3½	CM8-725	5.0	.115	Wire Term.	T-¾
53	14.4	.12	Bayonet	G-3½	CM8-801	5.0	.06	Min. Bayonet	T-3¼
55	7.0	2 c.p.	Bayonet	G-4½	CM8-802	5.0	.06	Min. Bayonet	T-3¼
55C	55	.050	Tel. Slide	T-2	CM8-803	5.0	.115	Min. Bayonet	T-3¼
57	14	2 c.p.	Bayonet	G-4½	1133	6.2	3.91	S.C. Bayonet	RP-N
63	6-8	3 c.p.	S.C. Bayonet	G-6	1252	24	.23	D.C. Bayonet	G-6
67	13.5	4 c.p.	S.C. Bayonet	G-6	1383	12	20w	S.C. Bayonet	R-12
67K	13.5	4 c.p.	Cand. Screw	G-6	1445	18	.15	Bayonet	G-3½
81	6-8	6 c.p.	S.C. Bayonet	G-6	1446	12	.20	Screw	G-3½
82	6-8	6 c.p.	D.C. Bayonet	G-6	1447	1.80	.15	Screw	G-3½

103

Table 1. Incandescent Lamps Cont'd.

Mfr's Type	Volts	Amps	Base	Bulb Style	Mfr's Type	Volts	Amps	Base	Bulb Style
93	12.8	1.04	S.C. Bayonet	S-8	1458	20	.25	Bayonet	G-5
112	1.2	.22	Screw	TL-3	1474	14	.17	Screw	T-3
137	6.3	.25	Min. Bay.	G-3½	1477	24	.17	Screw	T-3
157	5.8	1.1	Screw	G-6	1487	12-16	.20	Screw	T-3¼
158	12	.24	Wedge	T-3¼	1488	14	.15	Bayonet	T-3¼
159	6.3	.15	Wedge	T-3¼	1490	3.2	0.16	Bayonet	T-3¼
222	2.2	.25	Screw	TL-3	1493	6.5	2.75	D.C. Bayonet	S-8
223	2.2	.25	Screw	FE-3¾	1630	6.5	2.75	D.C. Pref.	S-8
224	2.15	.22	Special	TL-2¾	1768	6	.20	Midget Screw	T-1¾
233	2.3	.27	Screw	G-3½	1769	2.5	.20	Midget Screw	T-1¾
240	6.3	.36	Bayonet	T-3¼	1813	14.4	.10	Min. Bayonet	T-3¼
248	2.5	.80	Screw	G-5½	1815	12-16	.20	Min. Bayonet	T-3¼
259	6.3	.25	Wedge	T-3¼	1816	13	.33	Min. Bayonet	T-3¼
307	28	.67	S.C. Bayonet	S-8	1819	28	.04	Min. Bayonet	T-3¼
313	28	.17	Bayonet	T-3¼	1820	28	.10	Min. Bayonet	T-3¼
324	3	.19	Wire Term.	T-1¼	1822	36	.10	Min. Bayonet	T-3¼
327	28	.04	Mid. Flanged	T-1¾	1828	37.5	.05	Min. Bayonet	T-3¼
CM327LSV	2.80	.06	Mid. Flanged	T-1¾	1829	28	.07	Min. Bayonet	T-3¼
328	6	.20	Mid. Flanged	T-1¾	1835	55	.05	Min. Bayonet	T-3¼
330	14	.08	Mid. Flanged	T-1¾	1847	6.3	.15	Min. Bayonet	T-3¼
331	1.35	.06	Mid. Flanged	T-1¾	CM-1866	6.3	.25	Bayonet	T-3¼
334	28.0	.04	Mid. Flanged	T-1¾	1869	10	.014	Wire Term.	T-1¾
337	6	.20	S.C. Mid F	T-1¾	1891	12.0	0.24	Min. Bayonet	T-3¼
338	2.7	.06	Mid. Flanged	T-1¾	1892	14.0	0.12	Min. Bayonet	T-3¼
344	10	.014	Mid. Flanged	T-1¾	2128	3	.0125	Wire Term.	T-1
345	6	.04	Mid. Flanged	T-1¾	2180	6.3	.04	Wire Term.	T-1¾
346	18	.04	S.C. Mid F	T-1¾	2181	6.3	.20	Wire Term.	T-1¾
363	14	.20	Bayonet	G-3½	2182	14	0.8	Wire Term.	T-1¾

differing types of bases. The characteristics of the most popular types of incandescent indicator lamps are listed in Table 1. The bulb shapes and base types referred to in the table are illustrated in Fig. 10.

The voltage and current ratings are applicable after the lamp filament has reached operating temperature. When the filament is cold, its resistance is much lower than when it is heated. Therefore, the current through an incandescent lamp is very much higher than its normal current when voltage is first applied. This in-rush current, which can be 12 to 18 times the rated current, should be taken into consideration when designing an indicator system. Fig. 11 shows this phenomenon.

Neon lamps are also widely used as status-indicator lamps. A neon lamp requires approximately 60 volts to make it ignite.

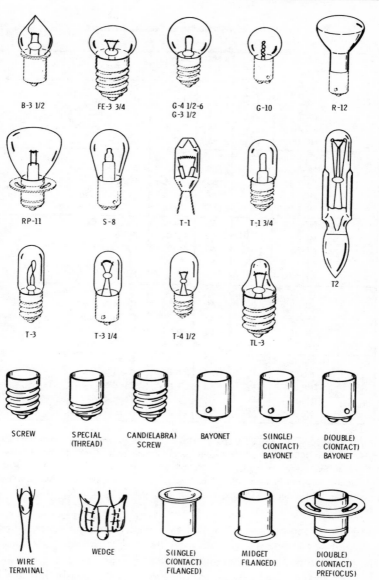

B-3 1/2 FE-3 3/4 G-4 1/2-6 / G-3 1/2 G-10 R-12

RP-11 S-8 T-1 T-1 3/4 T2

T-3 T-3 1/4 T-4 1/2 TL-3

SCREW SPECIAL (THREAD) CAND(ELABRA) SCREW BAYONET S(INGLE) C(ONTACT) BAYONET D(OUBLE) C(ONTACT) BAYONET

WIRE TERMINAL WEDGE S(INGLE) C(ONTACT) F(LANGED) MIDGET F(LANGED) D(OUBLE) C(ONTACT) PREF(OCUS)

Fig. 10. Examples of incandescent indicator-lamp bases.

105

Table 2. Miniature Neon Lamps

Mfr's Type	Watts	*AC V.	Bulb Style	Base
A1B	$\frac{1}{17}$	65	T-2	Wire Term.
†A1C	$\frac{1}{17}$	95	T-2	Wire Term.
NE-2	$\frac{1}{17}$	65	T-2	Wire Term.
NE-2D	$\frac{1}{15}$	65	T-2	S.C. Mid. Flange
NE-2E	$\frac{1}{10}$	65	T-2	Wire Term.
†NE-2H	$\frac{1}{5}$	......	T-2	Wire Term.
†NE-2J	$\frac{1}{5}$	105	T-2	S.C. Mid. Flange
NE-7	$\frac{1}{4}$	55	T-4½	Wire Term.
NE-16	$\frac{1}{4}$	§67	T-4½	D.C. Bay. Cand.
NE-17	$\frac{1}{4}$	55	T-4½	D.C. Bay. Cand.
NE-21	$\frac{1}{4}$	55	T-4½	S.C. Bay. Cand.
NE-30	1	60	G-10	Edison
NE-32	1	60	G-10	D.C. Bay. Cand.
NE-34	2	60	S-14	Edison
NE-40	3	60	S-14	Edison
NE-42	3	60	S-14	Sk. D.C. Bay. Cand.
NE-45	$\frac{1}{4}$	65	T-4½	Cand. Screw
NE-48	$\frac{1}{4}$	65	T-4½	D.C. Bay. Cand.
NE-51	$\frac{1}{25}$	65	T-3¼	S.C. Bay. Min.
†NE-51H	$\frac{1}{7}$	......	T-3¼	S.C. Bay. Min.
‡NE-56	1	60	S-11	Edison
NE-57	$\frac{1}{4}$	55	T-4¼	Cand. Screw
‡NE-58	$\frac{1}{2}$	65	T-4½	Cand. Screw
NE-66	1¼	65	T-4½	Cand. Screw
NE-84	$\frac{1}{4}$	95	T-2	Special Tel. Slide

For 105-600 v., except ‡210-600 v. §DC only. Screw types have series resistor in base for 105-125 v.; others require external resistor. In **Base** column of table, below Sk. means skirted; D.C., double contact; S.C., single contact; Mid. Flange, midget flanged; Bay., bayonet; Cand., candelabra. *AC starting voltage, DC starting v. 40% higher. †High brightness.

When a lower voltage is applied to a neon lamp, no current flows through it. A voltage greater than its ionization potential causes a neon lamp to become an electrical conductor and to emit a reddish-orange glow. Neon lamps have been recently introduced which produce other colors of light.

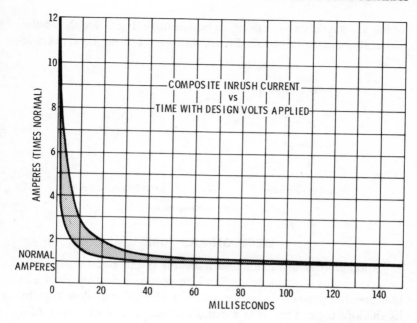

Fig. 11. Lamp current graph.

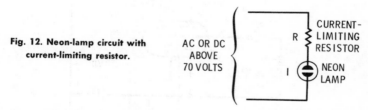

Fig. 12. Neon-lamp circuit with current-limiting resistor.

A resistance is usually connected in series with a neon lamp, as shown in Fig. 12, to limit the amount of current that can flow through the lamp. (Some neon lamps contain a built-in series resistor). Table 2 lists the most popular types of neon indicator lamps, and, again, Fig. 10 shows the various bulb shapes and lamp connectors.

Another popular type of indicator lamp is the light emitting diode (LED) which is characterized by extremely long life and

107

which are available in various voltage ratings. Fig. 13A shows the physical appearance of this device, and Fig. 13B is the schematic symbol.

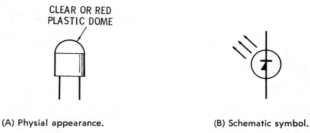

(A) Physial appearance.

(B) Schematic symbol.

Fig. 13. Light-emitting diode.

ELECTRON-RAY TUBE

Another type of illuminated indicator is the electron-ray tube (also known as the "magic eye") which produces a green glow and indicates the presence, absence, or level of a DC signal voltage by its shadow angle. Fig. 14 is a demonstration circuit of a type 6E5

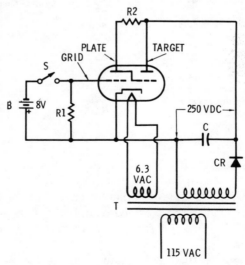

Fig. 14. Electron-ray tube demonstration circuit.

electron-ray tube. When switch S is open, approximately 260 degrees of its round screen (target) gives off a green glow, as shown in Fig. 15A (the shadow angle is approximately 100 de-

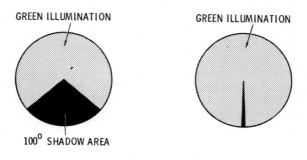

GREEN ILLUMINATION

GREEN ILLUMINATION

$100°$ SHADOW AREA

(A) No signal voltage.

(B) Signal voltage applied.

Fig. 15. Electron-ray tube indications.

grees). When S is closed to apply a negative DC voltage to the control grid (G) of the tube, the entire screen is illuminated, as shown in Fig. 15B (the shadow angle is 0 degrees). It requires approximately 8 VDC to obtain a shadow angle of 0 degrees. A lower voltage causes the shadow angle to be between 0 and 100 degrees.

An electron-ray tube can be used to indicate the presence or absence of an off-normal condition or the approximate level of a signal voltage.

ANNUNCIATOR

The electromechanical annunciator is an old-fashioned device used years ago in hotels, restaurants, and telegraph offices to indicate the source of a call for service. As shown schematically in Fig. 16, each identification unit employed an electromagnet which actuated a mechanical flag.

An example of an annunciator board is shown in Fig. 17. Each of the rectangles indicates either a "no" or "yes" status. Some

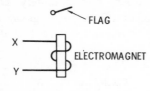

Fig. 16. Electrical circuit of an electro-mechanical annunciator.

1	2	3	4	5
6	7	8	9	10
11	12	13	14	15
16	17	18	19	20

Fig. 17. Example of an annunciator panel.

modern annunciator systems have similar display panels. Instead of a flag actuated by an electromagnet, each rectangle has a frosted-glass or translucent plastic window which is illuminated to indicate an off-normal condition. The window may be illuminated in differing colors to indicate various status conditions, or in a steady or flashing manner. The purpose of an annunciator panel is to indicate the location of an off-normal condition and, in sophisticated systems, the nature of the off-normal condition or request for service.

Instead of illuminated translucent windows or flags, many modern annunciators employ incandescent or neon lamps or LEDs (light emitting diodes). Fig. 18 is an example of the circuitry that can be employed in an annunciator employing incandescent lamps as indicators. In this example, the circuitry of only two lamps is shown.

When a remote NO sensor (*S1*) closes its contacts, relay *K1* is pulled in. Its 8-9 contacts latch the relay in the energized condition, contacts 5-6 apply power to indicator lamp *I1*, and contacts 2-3 energize the alarm buzzer. If the closure of *S1* was only momentary, lamp *I1* can be extinguished by pressing the NC push button *S3* to release the latching circuit. On the other hand, as long as the contacts of *S1* remain closed, *I1* will continue to glow.

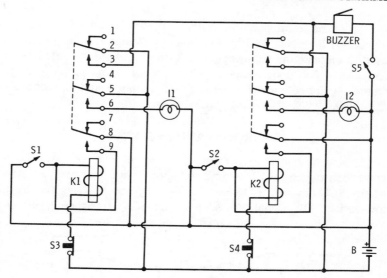

Fig. 18. Annunciator employing lamps as indicators.

Indicator lamp $I2$ is controlled in the same manner. Momentary or continuous closure of the contacts of NO sensor $S2$ causes relay $K2$ to be pulled in and to be latched into the energized position. The buzzer is actuated when either $K1$ or $K2$ is energized. It can be turned off, when desired, by opening $S5$.

Courtesy Barney Ephraim

Fig. 19. Commercial annunciator panel and alarm.

111

An example of a commercially available annunciator employing lamps is shown in Fig. 19. This particular display device is used to indicate the status of up to 24 doors. An illuminated lamp indicates which door is open. When a door is opened, when the system is armed, acoustic alarms are actuated and the door is identified.

ELECTRONIC ANNUNCIATORS

In lieu of relays, as previously shown in Fig. 18, the silicon controlled switch (SCS), a semiconductor device, can be used. Any of the SCS devices, as shown in Fig. 20, can be triggered by a low-voltage DC signal. As soon as an SCS is triggered, its as-

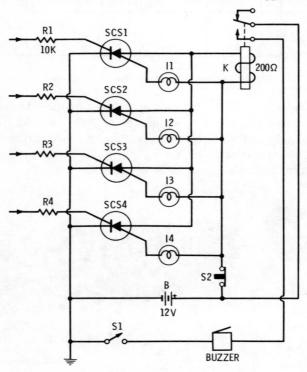

Fig. 20. Annunciator panel using silicon controlled switches

112

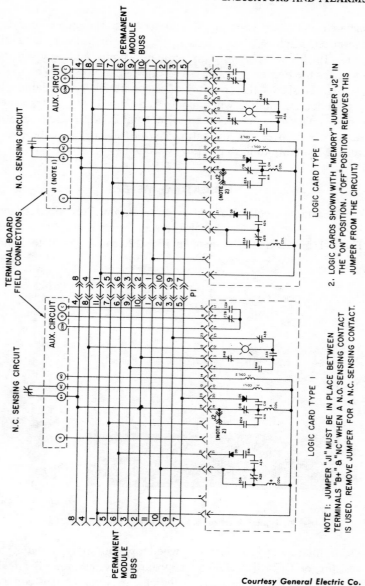

Fig. 21. Ciruit of a commercial plug-in annunciator module.

113

sociated indicator lamp is illuminated and the alarm buzzer is energized. Each SCS functions in the same manner as a latching relay. Each controls its own indicator lamp and any of them energizes the buzzer.

Fig. 21 shows the circuitry of a commercially available plug-in annunciator module which controls a lamp behind a translucent window. The module senses an off-normal condition and identifies the source as well as the nature of the off-normal condition by causing the lamp to flash or glow continually.

INDICATING METERS

An analog electrical meter (voltmeter, ammeter, or wattmeter) can be used to indicate the absolute or relative state of a sensor. The 0-1 milliammeter, shown in Fig. 22, can be used to indicate

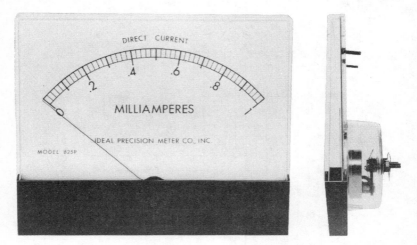

Courtesy Ideal Precision Meter Co., Inc.

Fig. 22. Typical direct current milliammeter with a calibrated scale.

DC milliamperes or amperes when appropriately shunted by a resistor, or DC volts when an appropriate series multiplier resistor is used. It can also be used to indicate AC volts when connected to a circuit through a rectifier and a multiplier resistor. To become aware of an off-normal condition, it is necessary to watch the meter unless external alarm circuitry is provided.

Most meters are calibrated in terms of voltage or current. When it is not necessary to know relatively absolute values, meters such as those shown in Fig. 23 can be used. The scales of these

(A) Rectangular shadow-type current or voltage indicator.

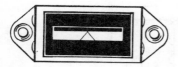

(B) Rectangular pointer-type current or voltage indicator.

(C) Rectangular zero-center status indicator.

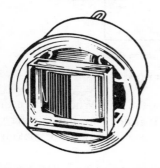

(D) Round zero-center status indicator.

(E) Round relative-voltage indicator.

Courtesy Radio Shack

Fig. 23. Example of meter-type indicators without calibrated scales.

meters indicate relative voltage or current level or deviation from zero voltage or current.

Examples of the uses of meters in alarm circuits are shown in Fig. 24. In Fig. 24A, a DC voltmeter can be used to indicate that the battery and relay coil are OK. When the NO sensor is open,

115

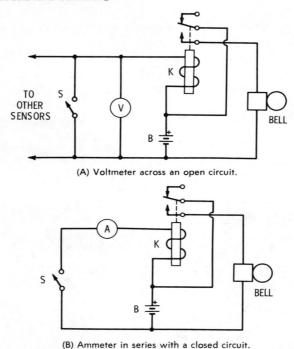

(A) Voltmeter across an open circuit.

(B) Ammeter in series with a closed circuit.

Fig. 24. Examples of using a meter in a sensor circuit.

the meter indicates that voltage is across the line. When the sensor closes, the meter should indicate zero. If it does not indicate zero, but less than when S is open, it could mean that S is not making good contact.

A DC ammeter is shown connected in series with one leg of the line running to an NC sensor(S) in the circuit given in Fig. 24B. Normally, the meter indicates presence of current. When the meter reading is less than normal, it can be an indication of impending battery failure or poor contact at S.

CHAPTER 5

Electrical Control
and Alarm Circuits

This chapter covers control and alarm circuits employing wire as the transmission medium and nonelectronic electrical devices.

BELL CIRCUITS

One of the most basic electrical circuits is shown in Fig. 1. Here, a bell is controlled by an SPST switch with NO contacts.

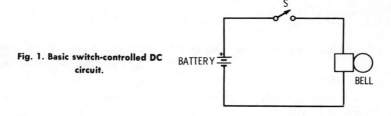

Fig. 1. Basic switch-controlled DC circuit.

BATTERY

BELL

S

The switch (S) may be a push button or other type of manually actuated switch. Or it can be a sensing switch whose contacts are closed when actuated by the opening of a door or window or by a person stepping on a mat.

117

A three-way bell control circuit is shown in Fig. 2. Switches *S1* and *S2* are both SPDT types. When both switches are in the

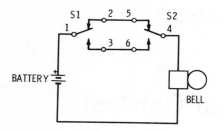

Fig. 2. Three-way control circuit.

positions shown in the diagram, the bell will operate. When either *S1* or *S2* is set to the opposite position, the bell ceases to operate. However, if both switches are set to the position opposite to that shown, the bell will again operate. The various possible switch conditions are as follows.

S1		S2		
Contacts open	Contacts closed	Contacts open	Contacts closed	Bell status
1-3	1-2	4-6	4-5	ON
1-2	1-3	4-6	4-5	OFF
1-3	1-2	4-5	4-6	OFF
1-2	1-3	4-5	4-6	ON

Instead of a bell, the load could be a lamp, siren, relay, door control or other device. In a practical application, *S1* could be actuated by an entrance door and *S2* by an exit door. When a person enters the room, a lamp or signal could be actuated and then shut off when leaving the room.

BASIC LOGIC CIRCUITS

A load can be actuated by an "OR" circuit when either of two switches or sensors is closed. As shown in Fig. 3, the bell can be actuated by closing either *S1* or *S2*. In the AND circuit shown

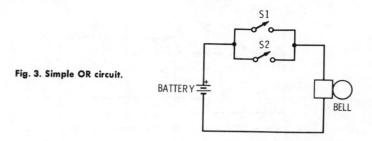

Fig. 3. Simple OR circuit.

in Fig. 4, the bell will be actuated only when both *S1* and *S2* are closed. In a security system application, the OR circuit is commonly used with two or more NO sensor switches in parallel. In the

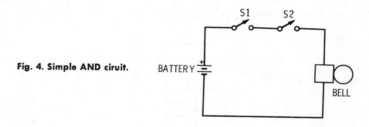

Fig. 4. Simple AND ciruit.

AND circuit shown in Fig. 4, *S1* could be an alarm on-off control and *S2* a sensor switch.

INTERPOSING RELAY

When it is necessary to install a bell at a considerable distance from the switches, particularly when a high-current bell is used, the voltage drop introduced by the interconnecting wires may be excessive resulting in marginal or non-operation of the bell. In such cases, a relay can be used, connected as shown in Fig. 5. The current required to cause the relay to pull in is considerably less than that required by the bell. When switch *S* (or any other NO switch connected in parallel with *S*) is closed, the relay pulls in causing its contacts 2-3 to close and allow current to flow through

119

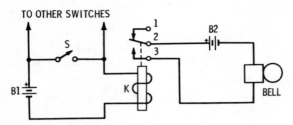

Fig. 5. Basic open circuit alarm system with relay.

the bell. Two batteries are used, one to operate the relay, and one near the bell and relay to operate the bell.

The bell stops ringing as soon as the contacts of the actuating switch reopen. The bell can be made to ring continuously until turned off manually by using the latching-relay circuit shown in Fig. 6. When switch *S1* (or any NO switch connected across it) is

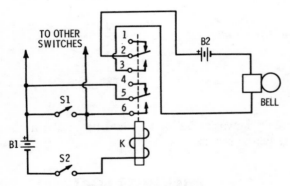

Fig. 6. Self-latching relay circuit.

closed momentarily, the relay pulls in. It remains pulled in because its contacts 5-6 close and apply a short circuit across *S1*. The bell rings continuously since relay contacts 2-3 are also held closed. To unlatch the relay and to turn off the bell, push button *S2* is operated to momentarily open its normally closed contacts. This releases the relay and contacts 5-6 open, removing the short across *S1*.

Another latching circuit, employing only one battery, is shown in Fig. 7. When *S1* (or any other NO switch connected across it)

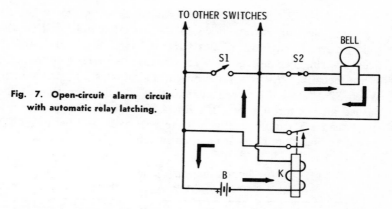

Fig. 7. Open-circuit alarm circuit with automatic relay latching.

is closed, relay K is pulled in and its contacts close to allow current through the bell. The relay remains energized after $S1$ has opened because electron current flows through the circuit as indicated by the arrows. The relay can be released and the bell shut off by momentarily opening normally closed switch $S2$.

SELECTIVE ALARM CONTROL

Two bells or other alarm devices can be controlled independently through a single alarm circuit when using the circuit shown in Fig. 8. Each bell is operated by its own battery. Bell 1 is controlled by $S1$ (and any other NO switches connected across it)

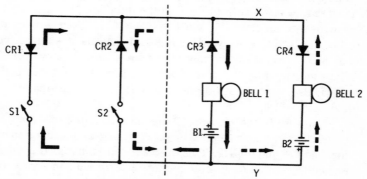

Fig. 8. Polarity-sensitive dual alarm circuit.

and Bell 2 by *S2* (and any other NO switches across it). When *S1* is closed, electron current flows in the direction indicated by the solid arrows through *S1*, diodes *CR1* and *CR3* and bell 1. Bell 2 does not ring because point *X* is negative with respect to point *Y* and because *CR4* is reverse biased and acts as an open switch. When *S2* is closed, electron current flows in the direction of the dashed arrows through bell 2, *CR4*, *CR2* and *S2*. Bell 1 does not ring because *X* is now positive with respect to *Y*, and because *CR3* is reverse biased and acts as an open switch.

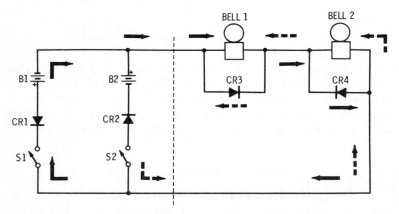

Fig. 9. Polarity-sensitive dual alarm circuit with diodes shunted across bells.

The bells can be connected in series as shown in Fig. 9. When *S1* is closed, electron current flows in the direction indicated by the solid arrows through bell 1, *CR4*, *S1* and *CR1*. Bell 2 does not ring because *CR4* is forward-biased and acts as a short circuit across Bell 2. When *S2* is closed, electron current flows in the direction indicated by the dashed arrows through *CR2*, *S2*, bell 2 and *CR3*. Bell 1 does not ring because *CR3* is forward-biased and short circuits bell 1.

Caution: If both *S1* and *S2* are closed at the same time, the batteries will be connected in series-aiding and will discharge through *CR1* and *CR2*. This problem can be avoided by using higher voltage batteries and connecting a resistor in series with each battery to limit the current.

CLOSED-LOOP CIRCUITS

The circuits shown so far are "open-loop" circuits in which an alarm is actuated by closure of any of one or more normally open switches. An example of a basic open-loop alarm circuit is shown in Fig. 10. Closure of *S1*, *S2*, *S3*, or *S4* causes the bell to ring. An

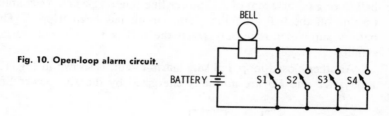

Fig. 10. Open-loop alarm circuit.

example of a closed-loop, fail-safe alarm circuit is shown in Fig. 11. Relay *K* is normally in the energized state with its 2-3 contacts closed and with lamp *I* glowing to indicate that the system is functioning.

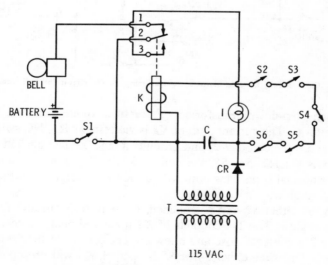

Fig. 11. Closed-circuit, fail-safe alarm system.

123

Electric power for the relay is obtained from the AC power line through step-down transformer T, rectifier diode CR, and filter capacitor C. Normally-closed sensor switches $S2$, $S3$, $S4$, $S5$, and $S6$ are connected in series with the relay coil. If any of these switches should open, the relay will drop out and its 1-2 contacts will energize the bell. The relay will also drop out and cause the bell to ring in the event of AC power line failure. Switch $S1$ enables turning off the bell after the alarm circuit has been tripped. The battery supplies power only when the bell is ringing, not during standby.

Another closed-loop, fail-safe alarm circuit is shown in Fig. 12. Relays $K2$ and $K3$ are normally energized by the AC power line

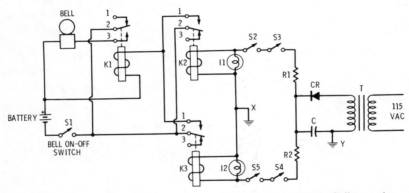

Fig. 12. Close circuit, fail-safe alarm system utilizing an OR circuit for bell operation.

through step-down transformer T, rectifier diode CR and filter capacitor C. The current path of $K2$ is via resistor $R1$, NC switches $S2$ and $S3$, the coil of $K2$, and grounds X and Y. The current path of $K3$ is via $R2$, $S4$, $S5$, the coil of $K3$, and grounds X and Y. Under normal conditions both $K2$ and $K3$ are energized and lamps $I1$ and $I2$ glow.

When either $S2$ or $S3$ is opened, $K2$ will drop out and $I1$ will cease to glow. The 1-2 contacts of $K2$ mate and energize relay $K1$ whose 2-3 contacts close and allow battery current to flow through the bell. Or, when either $S4$ or $S5$ is opened, $K3$ will drop out and $I2$ will cease to glow. The 1-2 contacts of $K3$ mate and energize relay *K1* which in turn completes the bell circuit. Relay *K1* is energized when either *K2* or *K3* drops out.

In the event of AC power line failure or breaking of the ground circuit at *Y*, both *K2* and *K3* will drop out and trigger the alarm. In case either of the line wires is grounded, the associated relay will drop out and trigger the alarm.

COMBINATION OPEN/CLOSED LOOP CIRCUIT

At a protected premise where both NO and NC sensors are used, the circuit shown in Fig. 13 can be used. The closed-loop

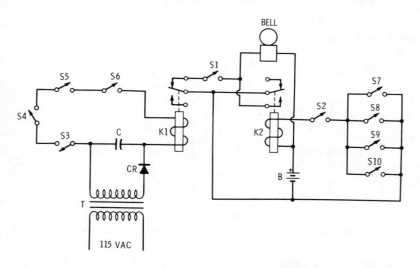

Fig. 13. Combination closed-circuit/open-circuit alarm system.

circuit relay *K1* is normally energized at all times by rectified DC obtained from the AC power line through transformer *T*, rectifier diode *CR* and filter capacitor *C*. If the AC power supply voltage should fail or if NC sensor *S3*, *S4*, *S5*, or *S6* should open, *K1* will drop out and its back contacts will complete the bell circuit. The bell can be shut off by opening switch *S1*. This switch is also opened when the closed-loop circuit is not needed.

125

The open-loop circuit relay (*K2*) is not normally energized. When any of the NO sensors *S7, S8, S9,* or *S10* is closed, *K2* pulls in and its NO contacts close and complete the bell circuit. Switch *S2* is opened to shut off the bell if necessary. By opening both *S1* and *S2*, the entire system can be shut off. Closing *S1* activates the closed-loop circuit and closing *S2* activates the open-loop circuit. With *S1* open or closed, relay *K1* remains energized as long as the loop circuit is closed and AC power is available. The power consumption of the circuit is negligible.

AC ALARM CIRCUITS

The *Alco FR-101* isolation relay can be used to monitor an open-loop circuit when connected as shown in Fig. 14. When any

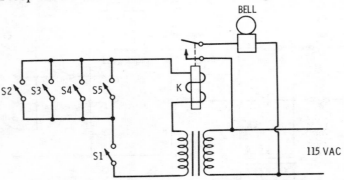

Fig. 14. Open-circuit alarm system employing an isolation relay.

one of the NO sensors (*S2, S3, S4, S5*) closes its contacts, the relay pulls in and applies the AC line voltage to a 115-volt AC bell or other alarm device. Switch *S1* is opened to disable the alarm circuit.

When used in a closed-loop circuit, the isolation relay (*K1*) can be connected as shown in Fig. 15. The relay (*K1*) is normally energized as is interposing relay *K2* (a 115-volt AC type). When any of the NC sensors (*S2, S3, S4, S5*) opens, *K1* contacts open and *K2* drops out. The back contacts of *K2* complete the bell circuit which is powered by a battery. The system can be tested

126

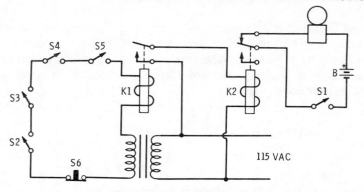

Fig. 15. Closed-circuit alarm system employing an isolation relay.

by momentarily opening NC pushbutton *S6*. Switch *S1* is used for opening and closing the bell circuit. When *S1* is open, the system is disabled, but a small amount of power continues to be consumed by *K1* and *K2*.

ACCESS CONTROLS

Access through a door can be controlled with an electrical door strike which can be energized by either AC or DC voltage. As shown in Fig. 16, the door strike can be actuated when a push

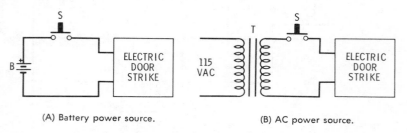

(A) Battery power source.

(B) AC power source.

Fig. 16. Electric door-strike circuits.

button (*S*) is closed to apply DC to the electromagnet of the door strike, as shown in Fig. 16A, or AC through a step-down transformer, as shown in Fig. 16B. The degree of security depends upon where *S* is located and who has access to it.

127

Control of the door lock of a private club, home, or industrial facility can be made more secure by employing a sensor which can only be actuated by plugging in an appropriately coded card. As shown in Fig. 17, the card reader is connected in series with the electric door strike.

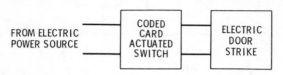

Fig. 17. Coded-card door-lock system.

A lock can also be controlled with a *Touch-Tone* telephone keyboard or a telephone dial. Instead of using a key, a person seeking entrance uses pushbuttons or operates a telephone dial. The circuitry of a lock controlled by a telephone dial is shown in Fig. 18.

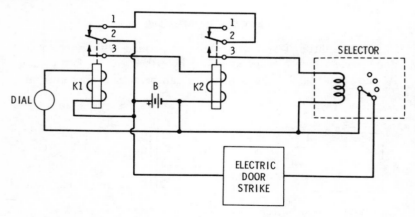

K2 = SLOW RELEASE

Fig. 18. Door-lock control system employing a telephone dial.

Normally, the telephone dial short-circuits the line when the dial is pulled (dialed from 0 to some other number). When the dial is released, it opens the short circuit across the line as many times as the number dialed. For example, when "7" is dialed, the circuit is opened 7 times.

In the circuit shown in Fig. 18, pulling the dial causes relay *K1* to pull in and its 2-3 contacts cause relay *K2* to pull in. As the dial returns to "0", *K1* drops out once for each dialed digit, but *K2* remains pulled in because it is a slow-to-release relay. As contacts 1-2 of *K1* close, DC is applied through contacts 2-3 of *K2* to the winding of the selector (*Secode* type 49-HS or equivalent). Each closure of the 1-2 contacts of *K1* causes the selector to advance one step.

If the selector is set to respond to the number 257, for example, its contacts will close and energize the door strike when that number is dialed. If any other number is dialed, the door strike will not be energized and the selector will return to its rest position.

CENTRAL STATION ALARM SYSTEMS

Typically, a central alarm station is connected through metallic circuits to its several protected premises. This is a closed-circuit system. In the event of opening of any NC sensor at any protected premises, an alarm condition will be indicated. Identification of a violated premises might or might not be indicated. When an encoder is provided at a protected premises, it will transmit a coded (on-off) signal which will identify the location.

A version of the famous *McCulloh* circuit is shown in Fig. 19. This circuit, which is very old, is still considered as a basic security alarm circuit. An alarm condition will be indicated if— the line is opened—shorted—or either leg of the line is grounded. It is a fail-safe circuit acceptable to most insurance companies.

There is a problem, however. Telephone companies are getting more reluctant about furnishing metallic circuits (DC) since the same pair of wires can be used as a voice circuit or multiplexed to provide a multiplicity of data or signal circuits.

When a telephone company is requested to furnish a signaling circuit, it may (at its option) furnish a metallic circuit (for DC transmission) or a derived circuit for transmission of on-off or coded information.

Because of this problem, many central station security alarm service companies are making greater utilization of tone transmission. They are also making greater utilization of electronic scanner techniques (see Chapter 9).

Although closed-loop DC circuits have inherent advantages, they are also "old hat" with respect to modern technology and are being gradually discarded because of the lack of availability of metallic circuits which will pass DC.

McCULLOH CIRCUIT

The *McCulloh* circuit is widely used by central station alarm companies in spite of its ancient vintage and in spite of the fact that there are more sophisticated techniques. Nevertheless, it has certain inherent advantages. It actuates an alarm when an NC sensor is opened and when the line is opened or grounded. One version of the *McCulloh* circuit is shown in Fig. 19.

Normally, line relay *K1* and ground relay *K2* are both pulled in and indicator lamps *I1* and *I2* are not lighted and the bell (or

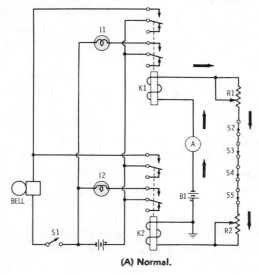

(A) Normal.

Fig. 19. McCulloh

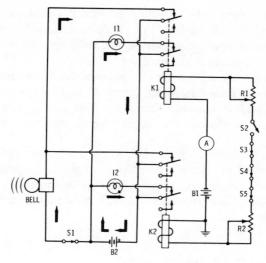

(B) Open sensor or line.

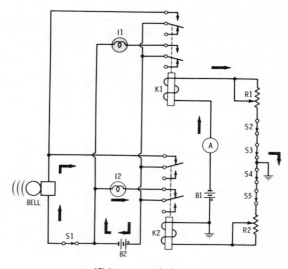

(C) Line grounded.

alarm circuit.

other alarm) is silent. The direction of electron current flow is indicated by the arrows in Fig. 19A. Potentiometers *R1* and *R2* are adjusted so that milliammeter A indicates approximately 10 mA or whatever current is required for security.

If the line or one of the sensors is open (as for example *S2* in Fig. 19B), both relays drop out, lamps *I1* and *I2* glow and the bell rings until *S1* is opened. The lamps continue to glow until the circuit is again closed. The milliammeter indicates zero line current.

Should the line become grounded, as shown in Fig. 19C, relay *K1* remains pulled in, but *K2* drops out. Lamp *I1* is dark, *I2* is illuminated and the buzzer sounds. The milliammeter indicates higher than normal current since *R2* and the winding of *K2* are no longer in the circuit.

CHAPTER 6

Electronic Control and Alarm Circuits

The demarcation point between electronics and electricity is vague. Both utilize electric current and both depend upon electron flow even if the electrons flow only through a wire. An electrical circuit can be said to be electronic when it utilizes semiconductors or electron tubes. Many so-called electronic security systems are actually pure electrical systems unless the use of semiconductor diode rectifiers in the power supply justifies the appellation "electronic".

Electronic circuits employing semiconductor devices (transistors, etc.) are usually assembled on printed circuit boards. A security system may employ several printed circuit boards which may be wired to external circuitry or plugged into a multiterminal connector to which the external connections are made. Fig. 1 shows a typical solid state alarm system module. The components are mounted on one side of the board and the connections between them are printed (in metal) on the other side of the board.

TRIAC CIRCUITS

The functioning of various electronic components used as switches was discussed earlier in Chapter 2. Among these was the

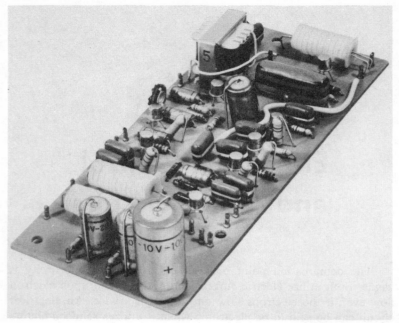

Courtesy Amperex Co.

Fig. 1. Example of a solid-state electronic alarm circuit.

triac, one of the most versatile and popular electronic devices where a significant amount of power is to be controlled. An example of an alarm circuit employing a triac is shown in Fig. 2. The NO sensors are connected in parallel and across the secondary winding of a 6.3-volt filament transformer (T). When none of the sensors ($S1$, $S2$, $S3$, $S4$) are closed, the primary of T has a high impedance and not enough current flows through it to trigger the triac. However, when any of the NO sensors are closed, the impedance of the primary of T is reduced and the triac is triggered into conduction and allows current to flow to the alarm device. Potentiometer R is used to set the triggering level.

Another example of an alarm circuit employing a triac is shown in Fig. 3. In this circuit, resistor R is connected to the gate of the triac through the contacts of relay K. This low-voltage AC relay is energized when any of the NO sensors ($S1$, $S2$, $S3$, $S4$) are

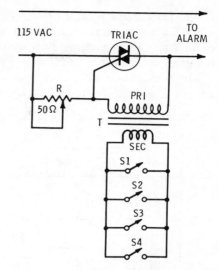

Fig. 2. Open-circuit alarm system employing a triac.

Courtesy General Electric Co.

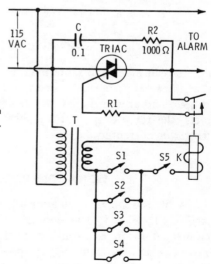

Fig. 3. Open-circuit alarm system employing a relay-controlled triac.

closed. Transformer *T* may be a 6.3-, 12.6- or 24-volt step-down transformer depending upon the rating of the relay coil. Capacitor

135

C and resistor *R2* form a protective filter which may be required when the alarm device presents an inductive load. The same type of filter may also be required across the triac in the circuit previously shown in Fig. 2.

In a closed-circuit alarm system employing NC sensors, the triac alarm control circuit can be wired as shown in Fig. 4. It

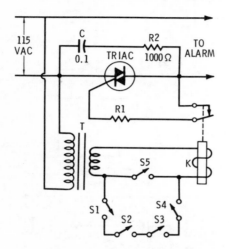

Fig. 4. Closed-circuit alarm system employing a triac.

operates in much the same manner as the previous circuit except that the relay is normally energized. When arm-disarm switch *S5* is open and any of the NC sensors (*S1, S2, S3, S4*) opens its contacts, the relay drops out and its back contacts mate and apply triggering current to the triac.

LIGHT-CONTROLLED ALARMS

A block-schematic diagram of a light-controlled alarm circuit is given in Fig. 5. The photoelectric cell or photovoltaic cell is connected to an electronic control circuit which drives a relay. Power is derived from the AC power line through plug *P* and is delivered to the alarm device through AC receptacle *J*. When light to the sensor is cut off, relay *K* drops out and its back contacts complete the circuit to the alarm device.

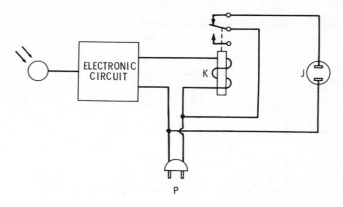

Fig. 5. Block schematic diagram of a light-actuated alarm system.

In the circuit shown in Fig. 6, a photo-electric cell is used in conjunction with a triac and a diac. When light impinges on the sensor, the triac is triggered and power is applied to the alarm device through AC receptacle J (or directly through wires). The light reduces the resistance of the sensor. When the voltage across the diac is increased to approximately 30 volts by reduction of sensor resistance, the diac conducts and applies triggering current to the triac.

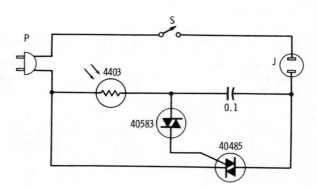

Fig. 6. Light-actuated control circuit which applies power to the load when light is present.

137

The circuit shown in Fig. 7 operates in the opposite manner. When light impinges on the light-sensitive sensor, the voltage to

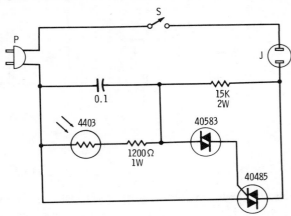

Fig. 7. Light-actuated control circuit employing a diac and a triac. Presence of light opens the load circuit.

the diac is reduced so it won't conduct and trigger the triac. When light is cut off, the resistance of the sensor rises and the voltage to the diac increases, causing it to trigger the triac which then passes current to the load.

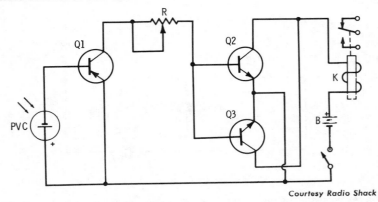

Courtesy Radio Shack

Fig. 8. Light-actuated alarm circuit employing transistors.

Transistors are used in the light-controlled alarm circuit shown in Fig. 8. The sensor is a photovoltaic cell which generates a voltage when it senses light. This voltage forward biases transistor *Q1* into conduction. This lowers the resistance between the collector and emitter of *Q1* which causes *Q2* and *Q3* base current to flow. This in turn causes the collector current of the parallel-connected transistors *Q2* and *Q3* to increase. This current causes the relay to pull in. The relay contacts can be wired so that an alarm is actuated when light is intercepted by the sensor or when light is cut off.

An electronic night light control circuit is shown in Fig. 9. A photoconductive cell is used to changed the forward bias on

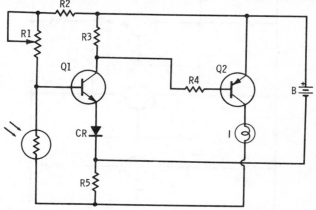

Fig. 9. Electronic night light circuit.

transistor *Q1*. When light reaches the sensor, its resistance decreases and the voltage drop across it is reduced. When no light reaches the sensor, its resistance becomes very high and the ratio of the voltage divider, composed of the sensor (PC), *R1* and *R2*, is changed so that the forward bias on *Q1* rises. The collector current of *Q1* which flows through *R3* rises. This increases the forward bias on *Q2* causing its collector current to also rise sufficiently to light the lamp. A relay may be used in lieu of a lamp and its contacts can be used to control an alarm device.

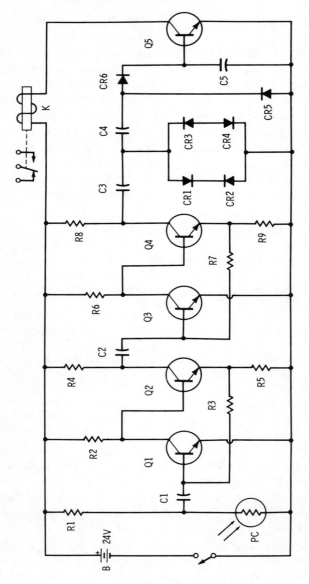

Fig. 10. A flame-flicker detector circuit.

A flame flicker detector circuit is shown in Fig. 10. It discriminates between a flicker and a steady flame. As shown in the diagram, there are four cascaded transistor amplifier stages followed by an amplitude limiting circuit employing diodes. The positive-going output signal is fed through a diode to a capacitor which limits the frequency response to less than 30 Hz. The voltage developed across the capacitor is fed to the output transistor whose collector is connected to a relay.

PROXIMITY DETECTOR CIRCUIT

A proximity switch that is actuated by touching or coming close to a sensor, which may be a metal plate, can employ an SCR as the switching device, as shown in Fig. 11. Normally, the SCR

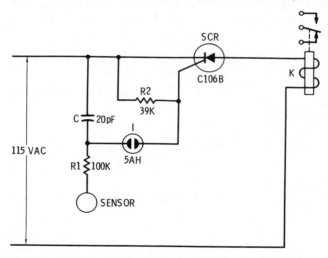

Fig. 11. Electronic proximity detector circuit.

does not conduct and the relay is not energized. When the sensor's capacitance to ground is reduced by the touch or proximity of a person, a capacitive voltage divider is formed in conjunction with capacitor C. The voltage across C rises sufficiently to cause neon lamp I to fire and pass a trigger pulse to the gate of the SCR.

141

Relay K is energized and remains energized as long as the capacitance of the sensor to ground is great enough. Since the power source is AC, the SCR is triggered once during each cycle.

The same circuit can be used in the latching mode by using DC as the power source. Once the SCR is fired, the relay will remain pulled in until the DC voltage is removed.

ELECTRONIC TIMERS

Most electronic timers depend upon the time constant of an R-C (resistance-capacitance) network. Fig. 12 shows the principle involved. When switch S is set in the charge position, current flows through resistor R until capacitor C becomes charged to the same voltage as the battery. When S is set in the discharge position, current flows through R until the charge in C is dissipated. The time constant is equal to the product of R in megohms and C in micro-

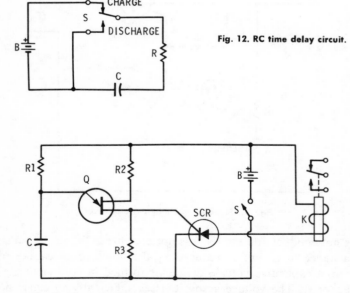

Fig. 12. RC time delay circuit.

Fig. 13. Electronic timer circuit employing a unijunction transistor.

farads. If R is 1 megohm and C is 1 microfarad, the time constant is 1 second. However, this is not the time required for the capacitor to become fully charged or discharged. The time constant is based on charging C to 68% of the source voltage.

Fig. 13 shows an application of the time constant principle. When $S1$ is closed, C charges through $R1$. The voltage across C is zero at first and rises slowly. When this voltage reaches the breakdown voltage of unijunction transistor Q, C discharges through the transistor and $R3$. The voltage developed across $R3$ triggers the SCR and the relay is energized. The relay is kept energized until S is opened. The charging cycle can be restarted by closing S. The time required for the charge in C to become high enough to trigger the unijunction transistor depends upon the

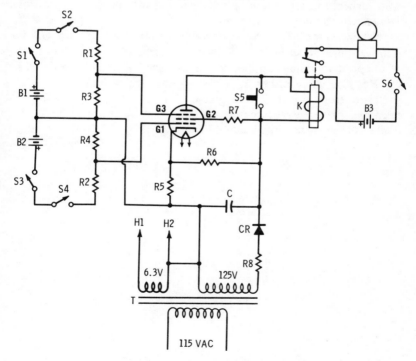

Fig. 14. Closed-circuit alarm system employing a gated-beam tube.

values of *C* and *R1,* the supply voltage, and the characteristics of *Q*.

GATED-BEAM TUBE ALARM DETECTOR

Because of the unique characteristics of the gated-beam tube (3BN6, 6BN6, 12BN6), it can be used as an AND gate and electronic switch. Since it is a fairly rugged tube, it is not as delicate as a signal-type transistor and can withstand some abuse. Fig. 14 shows an application of a gated-beam tube in a closed-circuit alarm system. Normally, all of the NC sensors are closed and apply positive voltage to grids *G1* and *G3* through the voltage dividers *R1-R3* and *R2-R4*. Since both *G1* and *G2* are positive with respect to the cathode, plate current flows through the coil of relay *K* which remains energized.

When either *S1* or *S2* opens, the positive voltage on *G3* is removed and plate current is cut off because *G3* is now negative of the positive voltage applied to the cathode by the voltage divider *R5-R6*. Or, when either *S3* or *S4* opens, the voltage on *G1* is switched from positive to negative. When either *G1* or *G3* is negative, plate current ceases and the relay drops out. Its back contacts then close and actuate the alarm.

CHAPTER 7

Security Communications

If Paul Revere had access to a telephone, he could have gotten his message across sooner to more people. Today, the backbone of communications is the telephone. City after city is installing the "911" emergency call system. To summon police assistance or to call for an ambulance, it is necessary only to dial 911 to reach an emergency dispatcher by telephone. Even some pay telephones have been modified so that 911 can be called without first having to deposit a coin in the telephone.

On the island of Jamaica, the emergency telephone number is 119 and in West Germany it is 110. In Wayne County, Pennsylvania the emergency telephone number is H-E-L-P (4357). While 911 may have been selected for technical reasons, 110, 111, 001 or 011 would have been a better choice since the caller could dial the number in the dark without wondering how to find the 9 hole of the telephone dial.

AUTOMATIC TELEPHONE DIALERS

Numerous companies manufacture automatic telephone dialers (Fig. 1) which can be actuated by a concealed push button, foot-controlled switch, or a fire or intrusion alarm sensor. Some can be actuated by a tiny radio transmitter. When actuated, the dialer

Fig. 1. A typical automatic telephone dialer employing a self-contained battery to enable operation without reliance on utility power.

dials the police emergency number or the telephone number of the fire department, sheriff's office, a telephone answering service, a security services firm or the person responsible for the security of the premises. After the called telephone responds, the machine plays a recorded message.

Many sellers of these machines state that the buyer will be able to alert the police directly. While the police in many communities will respond to calls from automatic telephone dialers, some police departments refuse to do so because they have received too many false alarm calls. This does not mean that automatic dialers are without merit. Arrangements can be made to have automatically dialed calls routed to a telephone answering service whose personnel in turn can call the police.

A telephone dialer can be connected to a telephone line through a wall-mounted telephone jack in the same manner as an extension telephone, or it can be wired permanently to the telephone line as

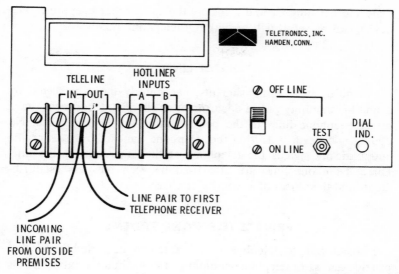

TELETRONICS, INC.
HAMDEN, CONN.

TELELINE
IN—OUT

HOTLINER
INPUTS
A — B

OFF LINE

ON LINE

TEST

DIAL
IND.

LINE PAIR TO FIRST
TELEPHONE RECEIVER

INCOMING
LINE PAIR
FROM OUTSIDE
PREMISES

Courtesy Teletronics, Inc.

Fig. 2. An automatic telephone dialer connected to a telephone line. The dialer is triggered by closing either A or B terminals with a remote switch or sensor. The B terminals, used for fire alarm, has priority over the A terminal.

shown in Fig. 2. Ever since the Federal Communications Commission made its famous "Carterfone Decision", telephone companies may not prohibit the connection of foreign apparatus (equipment not owned by the telephone company) to a telephone circuit. However, some telephone companies insist on furnishing and charging rent for a protective block through which the interconnection is made.

CALL DIVERTERS

Devices are available which automatically transfer calls from one telephone to another. In an unoccupied home or business establishment, such a device can lead a potential thief to believe that the premises are occupied. When the telephone number of the unoccupied premises is dialed, the call diverter automatically

147

dials another number and transfers the call to that telephone. The device can be set at will to dial any telephone number.

DIRECT LINES

Some business establishments, particularly those protected by a small-community police department or sheriff's department, have direct telephone lines to the police station or sheriff's office. No dialing is necessary. Lifting the telephone handset from its cradle automatically signals the telephone at the other end of the line. Direct telephone lines are also used between business establishments and the offices of a security service.

PRIVATE TELEPHONE SYSTEMS

In addition to telephones and a telephone switchboard that provide access to telephone company circuits, many establishments also have a private telephone system used only for in-plant communications. A private telephone system employing a manual or dial switchboard suffers from the same limitations as a common carrier telephone system—time loss involved in dialing, pushing the buttons of a touch-tone telephone, or even worse, waiting for a human operator to connect one telephone to another—plus inability to get through when the called extension telephone is in use.

MAGNETO TELEPHONE CIRCUIT

Where immediate security communication is required, a separate security telephone system can be installed. The simplest is a "hot line" system employing magneto telephones connected together on a party-line basis, as shown in Fig. 3. A person at any telephone can communicate with another person at any other telephone connected to the system.

To initiate a call, the caller cranks the magneto (an electric generator) which causes the bell at each telephone on the line to ring. To signal a specific person or telephone, the magneto is cranked to ring the bells in a coded fashion. For example, Jones

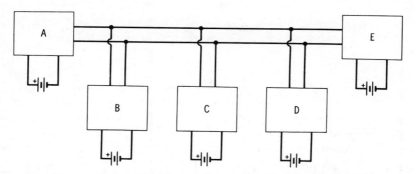

Fig. 3. Party-line telephone system employing magneto telephones. Each telephone is energized by its own local battery.

picks up the nearest hot line telephone when he hears two short rings and one long ring. Smith responds to one short ring and two long rings, and so on. In an emergency when all security personnel are to be alerted, one long continuous ring or a series of short rings can be used as the signal.

Before the magneto is cranked, a person wanting to place a call should pick up the telephone handset and listen to determine if the line is busy. If it is busy, the caller should wait or ask for the use of the line. If the line is not busy or when those using the line hang up, the caller should also hang up before cranking the magneto. Otherwise, the called and all others listening in on the line will be subjected to ear-splitting noise through the handset.

The telephones used in this kind of system are of the local-battery type. Each is connected to a set of dry batteries which provides the talking currents for the carbon transmitter (microphone). (A telephone company circuit is of the common-battery type. The talking current is provided by a battery at the switchboard or central office.)

SOUND-POWERED TELEPHONE CIRCUIT

A sound-powered telephone does not require a local battery. The transmitter (microphone) element of the handset is of the magnetic type; it generates an AC voltage when it picks up sound waves. A number of sound-powered telephones can be connected across a single-pair transmission circuit, as illustrated in Fig. 4.

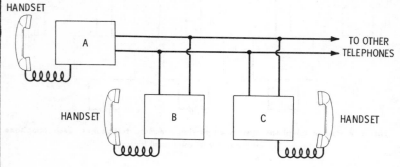

Fig. 4. Party-line telephone system employing sound power telephones requiring no batteries. Each phone contains a ringing generator and a hang-up switch.

Each handset is provided with a wall-mount hanger containing a switch that disconnects the handset from the line when not in use. Otherwise, there will be a significant drop in volume level because of the loading effect of each telephone when more than 12 telephones are off-hook simultaneously.

A ringing generator and bell are contained in each handset holder to be used for party-line ringing. The advantage of a sound-powered telephone system for security communications is that it will remain operational in case of electric power failure and does not depend upon batteries.

VOICE SCRAMBLERS

Since telephone lines can be tapped, privacy of telephone conversations is not assured. To enhance the security of telephone conversations, voice scramblers can be used. A portable voice scrambler that does not have to be physically connected to a telephone line is shown in Fig. 5. A call is placed by dialing or pushing touch-tone buttons. When the call is answered at a distant telephone, the handset of the regular telephone is placed in the acoustic coupler of the scrambler and its handset is used when

150

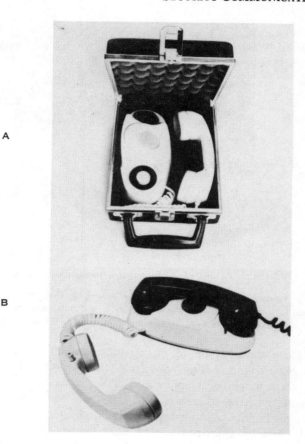

A

B

Fig. 5. Telephone set containing a voice scrambler. In telephone A, the instrument is shown in its carrying case. In telephone B, the instrument is shown ready to use. Conversation is carried on through the white handset.

carrying on a scrambled conversation. Obviously, the person at the distant telephone also uses a scrambler in the same manner.

A voice scrambler that is connected directly to the telephone line is shown in Fig. 6. It can be switched to the scrambler or normal mode as required.

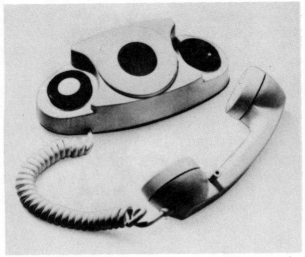

Fig. 6. Telephone set containing a voice scrambler designed for direct connection to a telephone line. When used in a dial telephone system, calls are initiated with a regular telephone connected to the same line.

The simplest type of voice scrambler merely inverts voice frequency signals. Rising voice frequencies lower in frequency and vice versa make them unintelligible. When receiving a scrambled conversation, the scrambler reinverts the frequencies and makes them intelligible. A wire tapper who understands electronics can easily hook up a device that will make the scrambled conversation intelligible. Numerous more sophisticated voice scramblers are available. Some can be set to any of several hundred scrambling codes.

Voice scramblers are also used in radio communications systems. Their use, however, is only lawful in specific radio services.

TELEPHONE LINE MONITOR

The occupant of a dwelling or business establishment is not aware of the fact when an intruder cuts the telephone line until an attempt is made to use the telephone. However, a device can be added (with the permission of the telephone company) which will sound an alarm when the telephone line is severed.

Normally, there is around 50 volts DC (from the central office) across the telephone line. When the telephone handset is picked up, this voltage drops to about 6 volts—it drops to zero when the telephone line is cut. A telephone line monitoring device senses the presence of DC voltage across the line. When this voltage is absent, it actuates a local battery-operated alarm. The device can be connected permanently across the telephone line or plugged into a telephone jack. A device of this type must be designed so that it does not load down the telephone circuit so that an off-hook condition will be indicated to the central office and so that it won't be damaged or triggered by the ringing voltage.

WIRELESS INTERCOM

Additional wires do not have to be installed to provide a communications path between wireless intercom units. Existing electrical power circuits serve as the "carrier current" signal transmission medium for almost any number of wireless intercom units.

Each intercom unit is a low-power radio transceiver operating at a radio frequency between 50 and 1600 kHz. Operation is on a single-frequency simplex basis as illustrated in Fig. 7. When station 1 transmits, station 2 receives, as shown in Fig. 7A. Then station 2 transmits and station 1 receives, as shown in Fig. 7B.

In the typical wireless intercom unit, a built-in loudspeaker functions as a microphone when transmitting and as a loudspeaker when receiving. A press-to-talk switch is used for converting the device from a receiver to a transmitter, and vice versa, as illustrated in Fig. 8.

Instead of an independent antenna, the radio signal is capacity-coupled within the the intercom unit to the AC power line which acts as an RF transmission line. The radio signal is superimposed on the power current flowing through the line. Most of the RF energy is confined to the wires; very little of it is radiated into space.

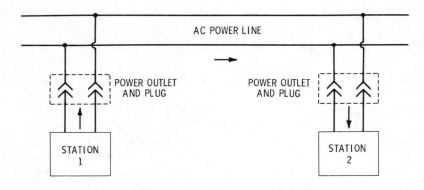

(A) Station 1 transmitting, station 2 receiving.

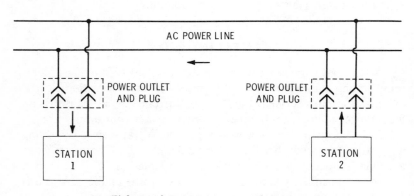

(B) Station 2 transmitting, station 1 receiving.

Fig. 7. Single-frequency simplex communication over a wireless intercom system.

When two or more wireless intercom units are used for inter-communication, all should be plugged into electric outlets which are linked by the same feeder line (not necessarily the same branch circuit). If there is a transformer in the line between the intercom units, excessive RF signal transmission losses might be introduced. When communication between two units is poor (weak signals or excessive noise), an improvement might result by reversing the poles of the AC power plug of either or both units at the electric outlet.

154

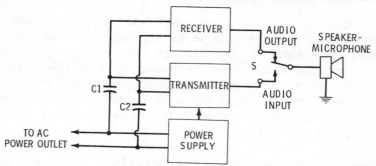

Fig. 8. Simplified functional block diagram of a wireless intercom unit. Switch S connects the speaker to either the receiver output or transmitter input. Capacitors C1 and C2 pass RF signals but resist flow of 60-hertz line current.

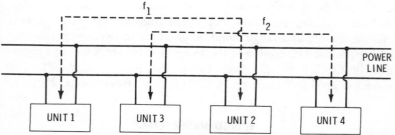

Fig. 9. Two or more independent wireless intercom systems can utilize the same power line as the transmission medium.

Any number of wireless intercom units may be used for communicating with each other when all are tuned to transmit and receive on the same carrier frequency. Two or more separate communications systems may operate, without mutual interference, over the same power lines when differing carrier frequencies are used, as shown in Fig. 9. (Transmit and receive frequency can be changed by internal adjustment of the intercom units.) In this example, units 1 and 2 intercommunicate on frequency f1 while units 3 and 4 intercommunicate on f2.

Some wireless intercom units can be locked into the transmit position so they can be used for aural surveillance purposes. For example, unit 1 can be set in the transmit position and all other units can be used for listening to sounds picked up by unit 1.

155

Most wireless intercom units employ AM (amplitude modulation) and are highly susceptible to electrical noise interference. More sophisticated wireless intercom units which employ FM (frequency modulation) are more immune to noise. Neither type provides secure communications, unless equipped with voice scramblers, since transmissions can be intercepted with a similar unit or an appropriate type of radio receiver connected to the same power feeder circuit.

In lieu of using the built-in loudspeaker as a microphone and sound reproducer, a telephone handset can be wired to a wireless intercom unit to provide some degree of privacy.

In spite of the marginal communications provided by wireless intercom systems in some electrical environments, they are flexible. Units can be quickly installed and moved from place to place without requiring installation of signal transmission wires. Transmission quality and range could be greatly improved by employing higher powered transmitters. By doing so, however, excessive radiation of the RF signals from the power line could result. The radiation level is limited by FCC Rules and Regulations, Part 15.

WIRED INTERCOM

A wired intercom system may consist of one master unit and one slave unit, one or more master units and a number of slave units, or it can consist of master units only. A master unit contains an AF amplifier whereas slave units have no electronic components.

A block diagram of a simple intercom system consisting of one master unit and one slave unit is shown in Fig. 10. Normally, as shown in Fig. 10A, the loudspeaker of the slave unit functions as a microphone and sounds picked up by the slave unit are heard at the master unit. To transmit from the master to the slave, as shown in Fig. 10B, the loudspeaker of the master unit is connected to the input of the amplifier, by means of a press-to-talk switch, and functions as a microphone. Sounds picked up by the master unit loudspeaker are reproduced by the slave unit loudspeaker.

156

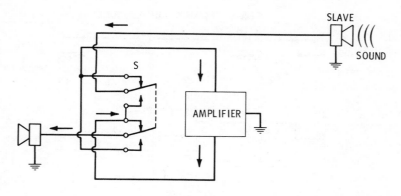

(A) Receive position.

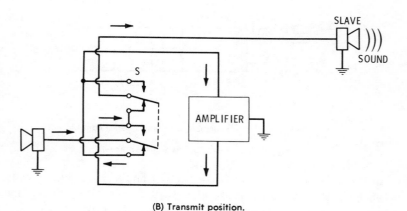

(B) Transmit position.

Fig. 10. Block diagram of a simple wired-intercom system.

The two units can be connected together through a parallel pair of unshielded wires (such as zip cord) as previously shown in Figs. 10 with satisfactory results. Electrical noise and hum pickup by induction can be reduced by using twisted-pair telephone wire instead of zip cord or its equivalent. Greater noise immunity can be obtained by using single-conductor shielded cable, as shown in Fig. 11A. The shield, which serves as one of the conductors, protects against electrostatic pickup of noise and hum.

157

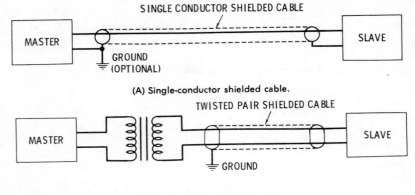

(A) Single-conductor shielded cable.

(B) Twisted-pair shielded cable.

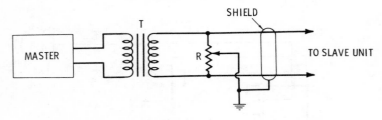

(C) Twisted-pair shielded cable with hum balance control.

Fig. 11. Wired-intercom transmission lines.

Even greater immunity to inductive and electrostatic pickup can be achieved by using shielded twisted-pair cable and a line transformer, as shown in Fig. 11B. The line transformer (T) is not required when the amplifier has balanced input and output terminals (neither side grounded). When a transformer is used with a master unit having unbalanced input and output terminals, it should provide the required impedance interfacing. The cable shield, whether used in an unbalanced circuit (A) or in a balanced circuit (B) should not be grounded except at the master unit end of the cable. In case hum pickup is still objectionable, a potentiometer (R) can be added, as shown in Fig. 11C. The potentiometer is used to balance the circuit and should be adjusted for minimum hum when receiving from the slave unit.

158

When the slave unit does not have a press-to-talk switch, persons in its vicinity are deprived of privacy since their conversations can be overheard through the loudspeaker of the master unit. For this reason and to keep the master unit loudspeaker silent except when reception from the slave unit is required, most slave units are provided with a press-to-talk switch. This switch can be bypassed or made functional by wiring it as shown in Fig. 12A.

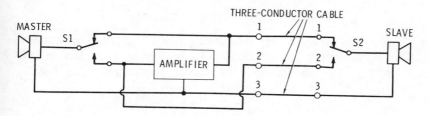

(A) Three-conductor unshielded cable.

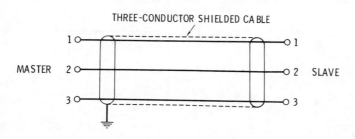

(B) Three-conductor shielded cable.

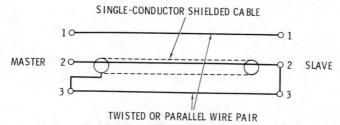

(C) Single-conductor shielded cable plus two unshielded wires.

Fig. 12. Transmission lines for slave unit equipped with talk-listen switch.

159

Three-conductor unshielded cable can be used to interconnect the master and slave units, as shown in Fig. 12A. However, when excessive hum and noise pickup is experienced, particularly from fluorescent lamps, three-conductor shielded cable should be used, connected as shown in Fig. 12B. In extreme cases, the arrangement shown in Fig. 12C can be used.

SELECTIVE WIRED INTERCOM

In a single-master/multiple-slave intercom system, the master unit has a number of push button or key switches for selection of slave units. As shown in Fig. 13, a separate two-conductor or three-

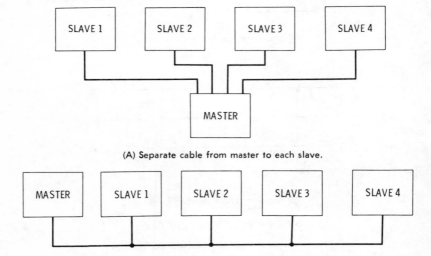

(A) Separate cable from master to each slave.

(B) Multiconductor cable with a separate pair or trio of leads to each slave unit.

Fig. 13. Single-master multiple-slave intercom system interconnections.

conductor shielded or unshielded cable is run from the master unit to each of the slave units, as specified by the equipment manufacturer and depending upon whether the slave units each have a press-to-talk switch.

A call is initiated from the master unit by selecting the desired slave unit and depressing the press-to-talk switch. A call is initiated at a slave unit by depressing its press-to-talk switch when one is provided.

Some master units are equipped with annunciators and are signaled from a slave unit by a beep tone and an annunciator which identifies the slave unit where a call is being initiated.

MULTIPLE-MASTER INTERCOM

A multiple-master intercom system may consist exclusively of master units, each capable of communicating with any of the other master units. Some systems of this type are capable of handling two or more conversations simultaneously. The master units are interconnected through multiconductor cables, as illustrated in Fig. 14.

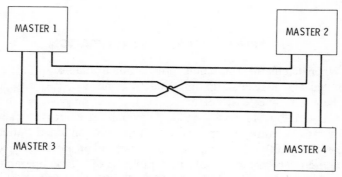

(A) Separate cables from each unit to each of the other units.

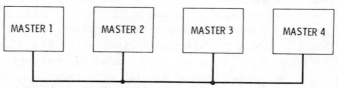

(B) Same electrically except all wires are contained within a single multiconductor cable.

Fig. 14. Multiple-master intercom system interconnections.

161

Slave units can also be used in multiple-master systems when the master units are designed for this capability. A functional block diagram of such a system is given in Fig. 15. A single-conductor

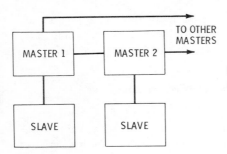

Fig. 15. Simplified connection diagram of a multiple-master intercom system with slave units.

shielded cable or an unshielded or shielded pair cable is required to interconnect a slave unit to its master, depending upon equipment design.

EMERGENCY RADIO COMMUNICATION

When telephone communication is not available, or has been disrupted and assistance or information is needed, two-way radio can be used. The least costly device for this purpose is what is known as a Part 15 walkie-talkie of which an example is shown in Fig. 16. Because its input power (from self-contained batteries) is less than 100 milliwatts, no radio station or operator license is required. The device should preferably be of a type operable on two or more channels within the Class D citizens band. It should be equipped to transmit and receive on Channel 9 (27.065 MHz), the official citizens band (CB) emergency channel and on one or more other CB channels. These channels are listed in Table 1.

To call for assistance, the walkie-talkie should be set to Channel 9 which is monitored by thousands of volunteers throughout the country, including members of REACT, a national organization of CBers (citizens band radio operators) sponsored by General Motors Research Corporation. After radio contact has been made with a CB station, the unit should be switched to another channel

Fig. 16. Low-power walkie-talkie which does not require a station license.

Courtesy Fanon/Courier

for continued conversations so that Channel 9 will be left clear for other emergency calls. The responding CBer will usually telephone the police, fire department or other agency when assistance is required.

Table 1. Class-D CB Radio Channels

Channel Number	Frequency (MHz)	Channel Number	Frequency (MHz)
1	26.965	13*	27.115
2	26.975	14*	27.125
3	26.985	15*	27.135
4	27.005	16	27.155
5	27.015	17	27.165
6	27.025	18	27.175
7	27.035	19	27.185
8	27.055	20	27.205
9**	27.065	21	27.215
10*	27.075	22	27.225
11*	27.085	23*	27.255
12*	27.105		

*May be used for interstation communications.   **Emergency only.

Ordinarily, it is unlawful for licensed CB stations to communicate with unlicensed stations, but it is permissible during emergencies.

More reliable emergency communication can be obtained with a higher-powered CB walkie-talkie (up to 5 watts input power), such as the one shown in Fig. 17, which must be covered by a Citizens Radio Service station license issued by the FCC. Better yet is a base station CB transceiver, such as the one shown in Fig. 18 which is operable normally from the 115 VAC power line or from a 12-volt battery when there is a power failure. The battery may be a 12-volt storage battery kept charged by a trickle charger or a pair of 6-volt hot shot batteries connected in series.

An external antenna, connected as shown in Fig. 19, will increase transmitting and receiving range. The CB transceiver can be left set to Channel 9 so that emergency calls from others can be intercepted.

Any U.S. citizen (individual, business organization or local government agency) is eligible to apply for a radio station license in the Citizens Radio Service. License application Form No. 505 and instructions for filing an application are available from the Federal Communications Commission, Washington, D.C. 20554.

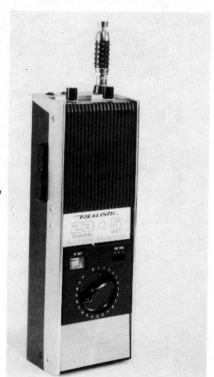

Fig. 17. Citizens band walkie-talkie
which must be licensed.

Courtesy Radio Shack

RADIO MONITORS

Householders, businessmen, and public safety personnel use monitor radio receivers for listening to weather information broadcast by National Weather Service radio stations throughout the U.S. These stations broadcast on either 162.4 MHz or 162.55 MHz, depending upon location. Receivers are available which are permanently tuned to a weather channel. Some are equipped with a decoder that actuates an alarm when a special emergency bulletin is to be broadcast.

Courtesy Pearce-Simpson Division of Glodding Corp.

Fig. 18. Citizens band base station transceiver.

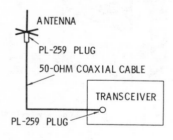

ANTENNA

PL-259 PLUG

50-OHM COAXIAL CABLE

TRANSCEIVER

PL-259 PLUG

**Fig. 19. Base station transceiver con-
nected to an external antenna through
coaxial cable.**

A weather news station can also be received with a tunable
monitor receiver, such as the one shown in Fig. 20, which can
be tuned to any channel within the 30-50 MHz, 150-174 MHz
and 450-470 MHz radio communications bands. Easier to use is
a scanner monitor receiver, such as the one shown in Fig. 21. Such
a receiver can be equipped for receiving on several radio communications channels. Unless set to receive continuously on a specific
channel, it scans the channels for which it is equipped, one after
the other until it finds a channel on which transmission takes
place. After the transmission ceases, the scanning action resumes.

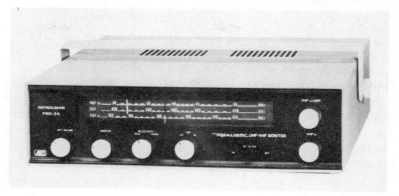

Courtesy Radio Shack

Fig. 20. Three-band tunable FM monitor receiver.

Courtesy Sonar Radio Corp.

Fig. 21. Scanner-type monitor receiver.

Receivers of this type are used for listening to the radio transmissions of local police, fire, and sheriff's departments in addition
to weather news broadcasts. These transmissions can be of considerable interest to an industrial security director since he can
be forewarned of criminal activities and emergency situations.
Although some police officials object to public interception of their
radio transmissions, many have indicated approval because they
receive valuable tips from listeners.

167

Monitor receivers are also used by civil defense workers and off-duty and volunteer police and firemen to intercept calls for duty transmitted by a public safety radio station. Some monitor receivers, designed specifically for this purpose, contain a decoder which keeps the receiver loudspeaker silent until a tone-coded signal is intercepted. The decoder activates the loudspeaker and also turns on a lamp. The lamp continues to glow until turned off with a reset switch. If the user finds the lamp turned on upon arrival at home, he or she will know that a call for duty has been transmitted and can then check by telephone to obtain the message.

RADIO PAGING SYSTEMS

Industrial security personnel can be alerted within a plant area or even many miles away through a radio paging system. Each

Fig. 22. Radio paging receiver.

Courtesy Kaar Electronics Corp.

168

authorized person wears a tiny radio paging receiver, such as the one shown in Fig. 22. Each receiver contains a decoder set to respond to its own code and, optionally, to an all-call code.

There are two basic types of radio paging receivers—one that issues a beep tone when it intercepts its code signal, and one that issues a beep tone followed by a voice message. When only a beep tone is used, the alerted person calls in by telephone to get the message.

The radio transmissions intercepted by these paging receivers are broadcast by a base station transmitter operating on the same radio frequency as the receivers. For city-wide coverage, the transmitting antenna is mounted on top of a tall building or on a tower or pole high above the average terrain. The transmitter is located near the antenna and may be remotely controlled from a distant point through a telephone line, as shown in Fig. 23.

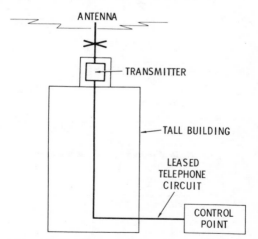

Fig. 23. Remotely controlled transmitter for large area coverage.

For short-range paging, as within a building or plant area, the transmitter may utilize slotted coaxial cable in lieu of a conventional antenna. This cable is connected at one end to the radio transmitter and is terminated at the other end in a 50-ohm dummy load. The cable acts as a continuous antenna which radiates radio

169

signals within the vicinity of the cable. In a long narrow building, the slotted coaxial cable can be run along the ceiling as shown in Fig. 24. In a larger building, two cables can be used fed through a power splitter, as shown in Fig. 25. In an open area, the cable can be supported by poles or suspended from a messenger cable and run in the shape of the letter C, as shown in Fig. 26.

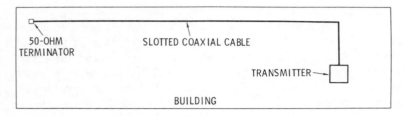

Fig. 24. Slotted coaxial cable antenna.

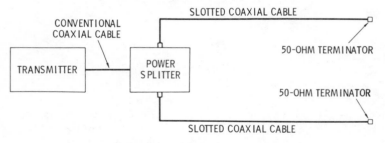

Fig. 25. Dual slotted coaxial cable antenna.

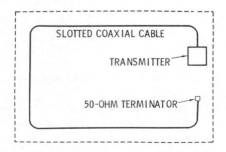

Fig. 26. Overhead view of a C-shaped slotted coaxial cable antenna for coverage of an open area.

When both in-plant and wide-range coverage are required, the far end of the slotted coaxial cable can be connected to a conventional antenna, as shown in Fig. 27. In this example, the cable

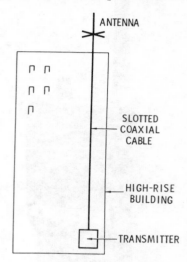

Fig. 27. Combination in-plant and large area antenna system employing an outdoor antenna and a slotted coaxial cable transmission line.

is run vertically through the floors of a multistory building to the antenna on the roof. The signals are radiated on each floor by the cable and away from the building by the antenna on the roof.

TWO-WAY RADIO

Many industrial security departments depend upon two-way radio for instant communication. Walkie-talkies, (such as the one shown in Fig. 28) are furnished to security personnel on foot. When vehicles are used by security personnel, these vehicles can be equipped with two-way mobile radio units, such as the one shown in Fig. 29. In some cases, vehicles are equipped with a radio system which utilizes a plug-in walkie-talkie. As shown in Fig. 30, the walkie-talkie is plugged into its mounting rack (and is connected to the vehicle's antenna and battery) when the security officer is in the vehicle. When he leaves the vehicle, he removes the walkie-talkie and takes it with him.

171

Courtesy Cook's Communication Corp.

The antenna is usually mounted on the roof of the vehicle, connected to the radio unit through coaxial cable, as shown in Fig. 31. The mobile unit is connected to the vehicle battery system through a two-conductor cable. The mobile unit may be installed under the dash or in the trunk. When a trunk-mount mobile unit is used, a control head, such as the one shown in Fig. 32, is mounted under the dash and is connected to the mobile unit through a multiconductor cable.

The walkie-talkies and mobile units can be used for communicating among each other and with personnel at a base station at the security office. The base station may be a desk-top unit, such as the

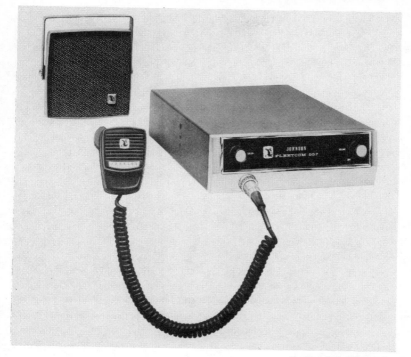

Courtesy E.F. Johnson Co.

Fig. 29. Two-way mobile radio unit for under the dash mounting.

one shown in Fig. 33, which is locally controlled. When access to the base station from other locations is required, a phone patch can be used, connected as shown in Fig. 34. When a phone patch is used, security personnel on foot or in vehicles can communicate with persons at any telephone connected to the telephone network.

An alternate to a phone patch is the installation of remote control units, such as the one shown in Fig. 35, which are connected to the base station through multiconductor cable.

When only plant-area communication is required, slotted coaxial cable can be used as the antenna, installed as previously discussed under RADIO PAGING SYSTEMS. This kind of cable intercepts as well as radiates radio signals. The use of this kind of antenna eliminates deadspots, particularly when communication

Courtesy General Electric Co.

Fig. 30. Plug-in walkie-talkie for mobile and portable use.

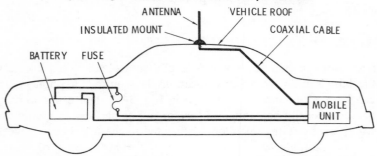

Fig. 31. Vehicle radio connections. The antenna is connected to the mobile unit through coaxial cable.

between walkie-talkies is utilized. When both plant-area and long-range communications are required, the slotted coaxial cable can be terminated in an antenna mounted on the roof of the building or other tall supporting structure.

174

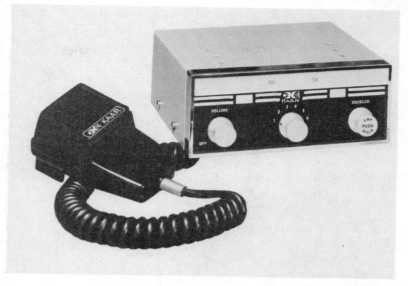

Courtesy *Kaar Electronics* Corp.

Fig. 32. Control head for use with a trunk-mounted mobile unit.

RADIO CHANNEL UTILIZATION

Most two-way radio systems operate on a single-frequency simplex basis, as shown in Fig. 36. In this example, both the mobile unit and base station are shown in the standby mode in Fig. 36A. Neither is transmitting. When the operator of the mobile unit presses on the microphone push-to-talk button, the mobile transmitter is turned on and a radio signal is transmitted to the base station, as shown in Fig. 36B. When the mobile unit operator releases the microphone button, the mobile *receiver* is turned on. When the base station operator presses the microphone button or operates a foot switch, the base transmitter is turned on and a radio signal is transmitted to the mobile unit, as shown in Fig. 36C. This is known as "simplex" operation since communication is sequential—one person talks while the other listens and vice versa. All units within range of each other can overhear all radio conversations.

175

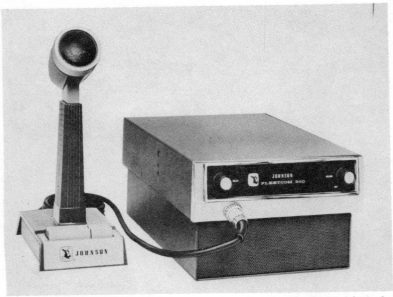

Courtesy E.F. Johnson Co.

Fig. 33. Desk-top base station.

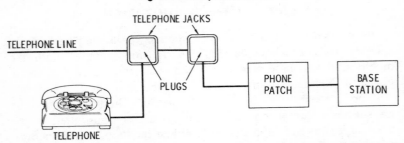

Fig. 34. Phone patch connections. The phone patch may be wired directly to a telephone line or plugged into a telephone jack.

In a two-frequency simplex system, a "paired" channel (two frequencies) is required. As shown in Fig. 37, the mobile units transmit to the base station on frequency f1 and the base station transmits to the mobile units on f2. All mobile units and walkie-talkies within range can receive the base station transmissions, but

176

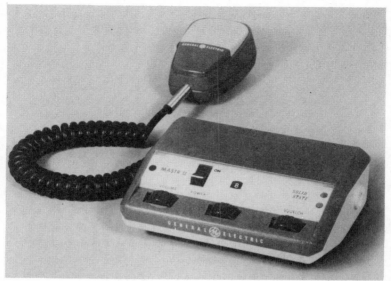

Fig. 35. Remote control unit for a base station.

mobile units and walkie-talkies cannot be used for direct inter-communication.

Communication between mobile units and walkie-talkies can be provided by utilizing the base station as a repeater station. As shown in Fig. 38, a repeater station is formed when the base station operator throws a switch that connects the output of the base station receiver to the input of the transmitter. Signals intercepted by the receiver on f1 are rebroadcast by the transmitter on f2. The block labeled COR (carrier-operated relay) automatically turns on the transmitter when a radio signal is intercepted by the receiver, but only when the operator-controlled switch is in the repeater position.

In the areas more than 75 miles from a metropolitan area with a population greater than 100,000, fully automatic (unmanned) repeater operation is permitted under an appropriate radio station license and when the repeater station is equipped to guard against activation by mobile units of another system.

177

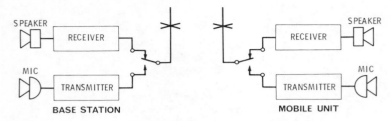

(A) Both stations in receive mode.

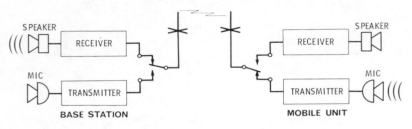

(B) Mobile unit transmits to base station.

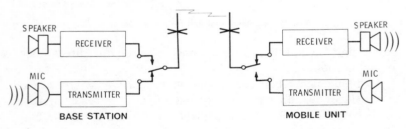

(C) Base station transmits to mobile unit.

Fig. 36. Single-frequency simplex radio communication.

RADIO CHANNEL AVAILABILITY

Radio channels for security communications are available within the 25-50 MHz, 150-174 MHz and 450-512 MHz bands. The hundreds of channels within these bands are allocated to various classes of users. Any business enterprise or local government agency is eligible to apply for a Business Radio Service license authorizing operation on one channel within one of these bands.

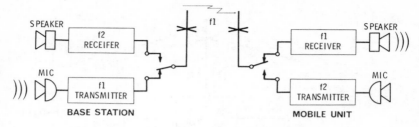

(A) Base station transmits to mobile unit on frequency F1.

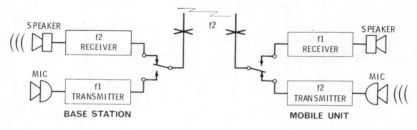

(B) Mobile unit transmits to base station on frequency F2.

Fig. 37. Two-frequency simplex radio communication.

Operation on more than one channel may be authorized by the FCC when adequate proof of need is shown.

Certain types of industries are eligible for licenses in the Special Industrial Radio Service. Various emergency organizations are eligible for licenses in the Special Emergency Radio service. And most local government controlled law enforcement and public safety organizations are eligible for licenses in one of the Public Safety Radio Services.

The channels available to these various services are listed in Volume V, FCC Rules and Regulations, which is available from the U.S. Government Printing Office, Washington, D.C. 20402. This book also explains how to apply for licenses.

Within the 26.96 - 27.26 MHz citizens band are 23 radio-telephone channels, previously listed in Table 1, all of which are available to all holders of Class D station licenses in the Citizens Radio Service. These channels may be used for both personal and business communications whereas the Industrial, Public Safety and

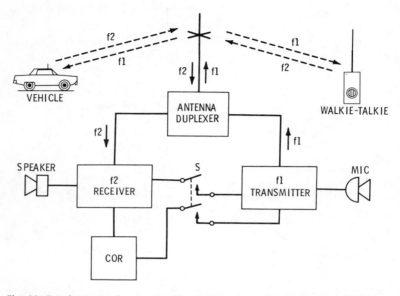

Fig. 38. Two-frequency base station, convertible into a repeater station by closing switch S. In this example, an antenna duplexer enables use of a single antenna at the base station.

Land Transportation channels may be used only for business and operational communications. The use of these channels for security communications, except emergency Channel 9, is not recommended because they are highly overloaded.

In addition, there are eight paired channels (16 frequencies) within the 450-512 MHz band which are available to holders of Class A station licenses in the Citizens Radio Service. Generally, only one paired channel will be assigned to any one licensee. These channels are not congested at the present time and should be highly suitable for security communications.

FREQUENCY BAND CHARACTERISTICS

The order of preference of the frequency bands for short-range security communication is as follows:

450-512 MHz band. Best from the standpoints of solidity of coverage (particularly within buildings), freedom from noise and immunity to interference from distant stations. Receiving and transmitting range is easily controlled. Equipment cost is greater than for the other bands.

150-174 MHz band. Very good coverage within most buildings. High immunity to noise but more susceptible to interference from other stations within a 15-mile radius. Range can be controlled. Equipment cost is less than for the 450-512 MHz band.

25-50 MHz band. Poor to fair coverage within buildings. Ignition interference from nearby vehicles can be severe. Interference from very distant stations can be troublesome, particularly at frequencies below 40 MHz. Transmitting range can be readily controlled, but receiving range cannot. Equipment cost is lowest, particularly for use within the 26.96-35 MHz range.

VOICE-PLUS COMMUNICATION

Ordinarily, only voice communication is used in non-government security operations. However, there is a gradual trend toward supplementation of voice communication with hard-copy and coded communication.

For example, emergency vehicles are being equipped with hard-copy readout devices. When a vehicle is not occupied, a hard-copy (facsimile or teleprinter) message can be transmitted which can be read when the vehicle is occupied. This kind of system requires the installation of a teletypewriter or facsimile transmitter at the dispatch center and a teleprinter or facsimile receiver in the vehicle.

Coded radio signals can be transmitted from a vehicle to the dispatch center or security office when the vehicle is equipped with an encoder, such as the one shown in Fig. 39. When time is of the essence, the vehicle operator pushes buttons to transmit a coded signal which is deciphered and recorded at the receiving station .The device also automatically identifies the vehicle (in a code) whenever the mobile transmitter is activated.

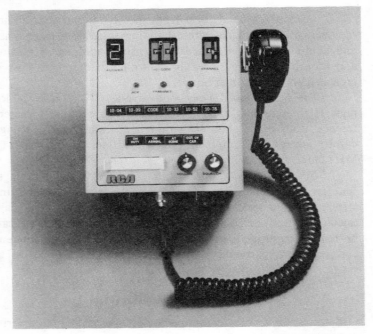

Fig. 39. Voice-plus control head.

Within a plant, only a single pair of wires is required for transmission of messages from any of several teletypewriters to all of the other teletypewriters connected to the same circuit. The same is true of facsimile transmitter-receiver units which can be used for transmission and reproduction of written and typed copy, drawings and sketches, and screened phtotographs. In a teletypewriter system, DC pulses are transmitted. In a facsimile system, analog signals within the voice-frequency range are transmitted.

LOW-FREQUENCY RADIO SYSTEMS

An FCC radio station license is not required for the operation of low-power radio transmitters which operate within the 160-190 kHz band. Part 15, FCC Rules and Regulations, limits transmitter input power to 1 watt and transmitter antenna length to 50 feet (including transmission line). These rules, however, do not limit the length of the receiving antenna nor the sensitivity of the receiver. The communicating range can be less than 100 feet or, as reported by experimenters, greater than 50 miles.

Although the 160-190 kHz band is only 30 kHz wide, it can accommodate at least three 8-kHz wide AM channels, six 4-kHz wide SSB (single sideband) channels, or one ± 15 kHz FM channel. Each of these channels can accommodate one voice or facsimile channel or 16 or more teletypewriter or slow-speed data channels.

Fig. 40 shows how a full-duplex voice frequency channel can be obtained. The carrier frequency of transmitter 1 is at 165 kHz

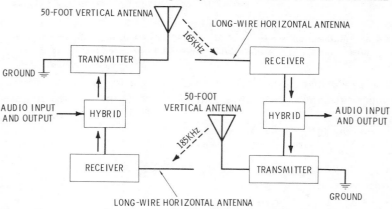

Fig. 40. Functional block diagram of a 160-190 kHz full-duplex AM communications system. The blocks labeled "hybrid" converts a 4-wire circuit to a 2-wire circuit.

and that of transmitter 2 is at 185 kHz. When both are amplitude modulated at frequencies up to 3000 Hz (3 kHz), 14 kHz of guard band space is provided.

Two full-duplex voice frequency channels can be derived by utilizing ISB (independent sideband) transmitters and receivers, as shown in Fig. 41. In an ISB transmitter, the carrier frequency is suppressed and both sidebands are transmitted. Assuming that the suppressed carrier frequency of transmitter 1 is 165 kHz, the

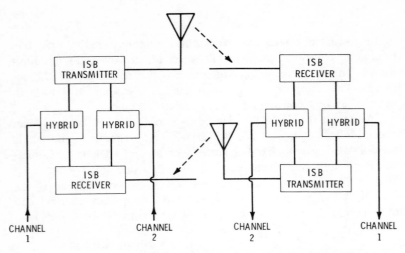

Fig. 41. Functional block diagram of the 160-190 kHz full-duplex ISB communications system. The blocks labeled "hybrid" converts a 4-wire circuit to a 2-wire ciruit.

lower sideband (LSB) will extend downward to 162 kHz and the upper sideband (USB) upward to 168 kHz. If the suppressed car-

ONE–WAY CHANNELS	KHz	DUPLEX CHANNELS
	160	
	162	EAST 1
1	164	
	166	WEST 3
2	168	
	170	EAST 2
3	172	
	174	WEST 2
4	176	
	178	EAST 3
5	180	
	182	WEST 1
6	184	
	186	
	188	
	190	

Fig. 42. Example of 160-190 kHz band spectrum utilization for SSB transmission. At left, six one-way channels spaced 4 kHz. At right, three two-way channels.

184

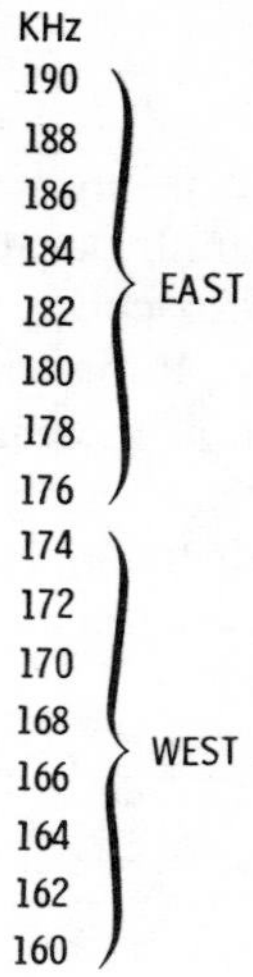

```
KHz
190 ⎫
188 ⎪
186 ⎪
184 ⎬ EAST
182 ⎪
180 ⎪
178 ⎪
176 ⎭
174 ⎫
172 ⎪
170 ⎪
168 ⎬ WEST
166 ⎪
164 ⎪
162 ⎪
160 ⎭
```

Fig. 43. Utilization of 160-190 kHz band for FM transmission (up to ± 7.5 kHz deviation). One channel can occupy the 160-175 kHz portion of the band. The second channel (in the same or reverse direction) can occupy the 175-190 kHz portion of the band.

rier frequency of transmitter 2 is 185 kHz, the LSB will extend to 182 kHz and the USB to 188 kHz. Again, 14 kHz of guard band space is provided which can be used for other purposes. Since each of the sidebands can be modulated independently, four one-way or two two-way channels can be derived.

Three full-duplex or six one-way voice frequency channels can be transmitted within the 160-190 kHz band when SSB transmitters and receivers are used. Fig. 42 shows how the spectrum can be utilized for SSB transmission . And, Fig. 43 shows how the spectrum can be utilized for conveying one full-duplex FM channel.

FCC rules do not prohibit the use of voice scramblers in this band, but the rules do prohibit the use of this band for bugging devices. Since the use of voice scramblers is not prohibited, the 160-190 kHz band can be used for secure communications.

Unlicensed transmitters may also be operated within the 540-1600 kHz AM broadcast band. Transmitter power input is limited to 100 milliwatts and antenna length (including transmission line) to 10 feet. Radio communications within this band can be readily intercepted with a conventional AM broadcast band receiver. Care must be exercised, when operating transmitters within this

185

band, to avoid interfering with the reception of AM broadcast stations.

Range is limited by the 10-foot transmitting antenna length and 100-milliwatt transmitter power restrictions. However, there are no restrictions on receiving antenna length nor on receiver sensitivity. Range in both the 160-190 kHz and 540-1600 kHz bands can be increased by: (1) increasing receiving antenna capture area, (2) increasing receiver sensitivity, and (3) reducing receiver bandwidth to improve the signal-to-noise ratio to compensate for high receiver sensitivity.

CHAPTER 8

Closed Circuit Television

A CCTV (closed circuit television) system may consist of only one camera and only one monitor or of a number of cameras and monitors and associated signal processing equipment. Some CCTV systems are much more complex than a television program production facility.

CAMERAS

Vidicon cameras are used in most CCTV systems because of their relatively low cost, small size and adequate performance. The name "vidicon" is used to denote that the camera employs a vidicon tube for viewing the scene. The vidicon tube senses variation in light sensitivity in somewhat the same manner as camera film. Unlike film which sees an entire scene at once, the vidicon tube scans the scene, as shown in Fig. 1, and divides it into hundreds of horizontal lines. It converts light variations into an electrical signal known as a "video" signal which contains frequencies ranging up to several megahertz.

While most vidicon cameras require fairly bright lighting, there are low light level cameras that work even under starlight and infrared cameras that work when the scene is illuminated by invisible infrared rays.

187

LIGHT SENSITIVE AREA

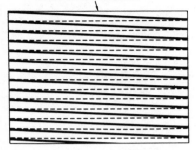

Fig. 1. Scanning action of the vidicon camera tube.

———— = SCANNING LINE WHEN LIGHT IS SENSED

- - - - = RETRACE LINE WHEN LIGHT IS NOT BEING SENSED

Courtesy Unimetrics, Inc.

Fig. 2. Example of a monochrome TV camera employing a vidicon tube.

Television broadcast stations, network studios and TV program production organizations use more expensive cameras which employ more costly viewing tubes. However, cameras employing vidicon tubes are also used by the broadcast industry, particularly in color cameras and in compact monochrome (black and white) cameras used for remote pickups and for viewing motion picture films.

The typical CCTV cameras, such as the one shown in Fig. 2, has a self-contained sync generator which synchronizes the scanning action of the camera and the viewing monitor. The video output signal (picture and scanning information), generated by the camera, is obtained at a female coaxial receptacle at the rear of the camera. The level of this signal is nominally 1 volt peak-to-peak and is intended to be transmitted through 75-ohm coaxial cable to a 75-ohm load, such as a video monitor.

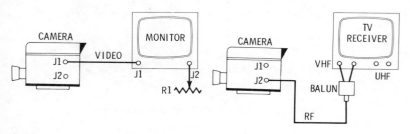

(A) The video output from J1 at the camera is fed through a 75-ohm coaxial cable to J1 on the monitor.

(B) The RF output from J2 of the camera is fed through a 75-ohm coaxial cable to the input of the balun whose 300-ohm output is fed to the VHF terminals of the TV receiver.

Fig. 3. Basic CCTV system.

Some CCTV cameras also contain a tiny AM (amplitude modulation) radio transmitter operating at one of the VHF television broadcast channel frequencies (usually Channel 2 or 3). Such a camera has two coaxial outlets, one for the video signal and one for the video modulated radio (RF) signal. In a basic CCTV system, the video signal is fed to the input of a video monitor, as shown in Fig. 3A or the RF signal is fed to the input of a conventional TV receiver, as shown in Fig. 3B.

Cables

In both cases, the camera is connected to the video monitor or the TV receiver through 75-ohm coaxial cable. In the latter case, a balun is used at the TV receiver antenna terminals to match the 75-ohm unbalanced coaxial transmission line to the 300-ohm balanced input of the TV receiver. A typical balun is shown in Fig. 4.

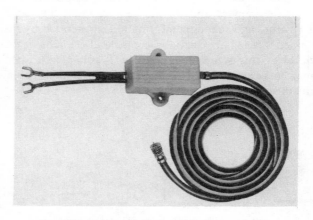

Fig. 4. Balun with a 75-ohm coaxial cable attached.

A balun is a transformer with a 4:1 impedance ratio and is called a balun because it interfaces a balanced (bal) circuit to an unbalanced (un) circuit.

Each end of the coaxial cable is terminated in a male coaxial connector. The steps for attaching soldered-type PL-259 UHF coaxial connectors to RG-11/U and RG-59/U coaxial cables are illustrated in Fig. 5. Solderless coaxial connectors are also available. Most cameras are equipped with type SO-239 coaxial receptacles which mate with type PL-259 male connectors. Some cameras, however, are equipped with other types of female coaxial connectors in which cases appropriate type male connectors must be used.

Broadcast type and more expensive CCTV cameras employ connectors for accommodating multi-conductor cables terminated in appropriate plugs.

190

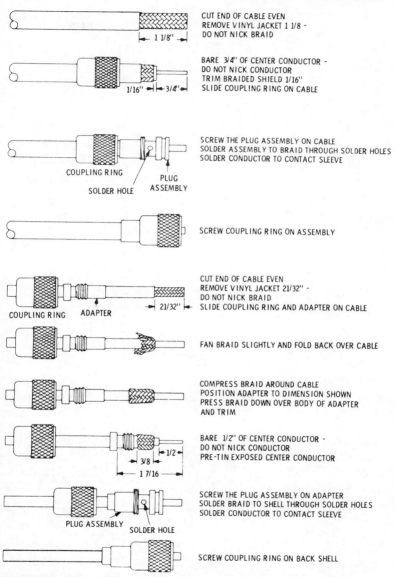

CUT END OF CABLE EVEN
REMOVE VINYL JACKET 1 1/8 -
DO NOT NICK BRAID

1 1/8"

BARE 3/4" OF CENTER CONDUCTOR -
DO NOT NICK CONDUCTOR
TRIM BRAIDED SHIELD 1/16"
SLIDE COUPLING RING ON CABLE

1/16" 3/4"

SCREW THE PLUG ASSEMBLY ON CABLE
SOLDER ASSEMBLY TO BRAID THROUGH SOLDER HOLES
SOLDER CONDUCTOR TO CONTACT SLEEVE

COUPLING RING

PLUG
SOLDER HOLE   ASSEMBLY

SCREW COUPLING RING ON ASSEMBLY

CUT END OF CABLE EVEN
REMOVE VINYL JACKET 21/32" -
DO NOT NICK BRAID
SLIDE COUPLING RING AND ADAPTER ON CABLE

COUPLING RING   ADAPTER   21/32"

FAN BRAID SLIGHTLY AND FOLD BACK OVER CABLE

COMPRESS BRAID AROUND CABLE
POSITION ADAPTER TO DIMENSION SHOWN
PRESS BRAID DOWN OVER BODY OF ADAPTER
AND TRIM

BARE 1/2" OF CENTER CONDUCTOR -
DO NOT NICK CONDUCTOR
PRE-TIN EXPOSED CENTER CONDUCTOR

1/2
3/8
1 7/16

SCREW THE PLUG ASSEMBLY ON ADAPTER
SOLDER BRAID TO SHELL THROUGH SOLDER HOLES
SOLDER CONDUCTOR TO CONTACT SLEEVE

PLUG ASSEMBLY   SOLDER HOLE

SCREW COUPLING RING ON BACK SHELL

Fig. 5. Method of installing a PL-259 UHF type coaxial connector to RG-11/U and RG-59/U coaxial cable.

191

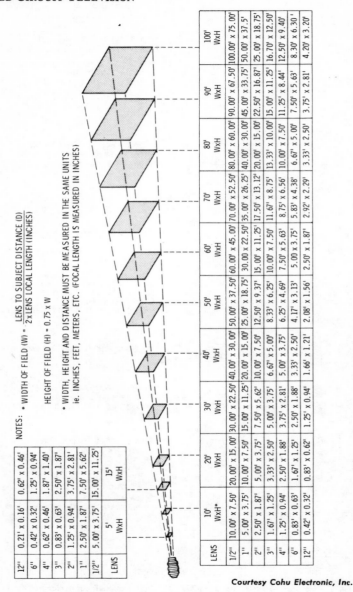

Courtesy Cohu Electronic, Inc.

Fig. 6. Lens viewing area for lenses of different focal lengths.

Lenses

A television camera may be equipped with only one lens or with a lens turret for accommodating two or three lenses. There is a wide choice of lenses for use with CCTV cameras.

As Fig. 6 shows, the area that can be seen by a lens at a specific distance depends upon its focal length. The amount of light a lens can pass and its depth of focus depend upon the rating of the lens. A zoom lens offers great flexibility since it can be used for observation of both close-in and distance objects. A lens can be focused manually when used for viewing only one specific scene at a fixed distance. When the same camera is to be used for viewing objects at various distances, electro-mechanical remote control of lenses and lens turrets can be provided.

PICTURE MONITORS

A video monitor is similar to a TV receiver except that it does not have a channel selector switch and does not contain circuitry for interception and processing of RF signals.

Fig. 7. Typical monochrome video monitor.

Courtesy Panasonic

An example of a video monitor is shown in Fig. 7. It has two coaxial connectors which are bridged together internally. When two such monitors are used with a single camera or other picture

193

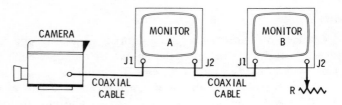

Fig. 8. Method for connecting two video monitors to the video output of a camera.

signal source, they are connected as shown in Fig. 8. The camera is connected to coaxial receptacle *J1* of monitor A through 75-ohm coaxial cable. *J2* is connected to *J1* of monitor B, also through 75-ohm coaxial cable, and a 75-ohm termination resistor (R) is plugged

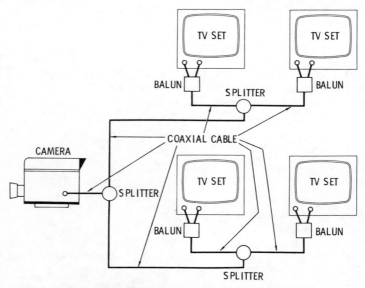

Fig. 9. Four TV receivers used as monitors can be fed from the RF output of a camera through splitters.

into *J2* of monitor B. The function of the termination resistor is to provide a 75-ohm load for the video circuit. If not so terminated, distorted pictures may result because of reflection of the signals which can occur when a circuit is not properly terminated. Some

194

monitors have a built-in termination resistor which can be bridged across *J2* internally by means of a switch.

Conventional TV receivers are often used as CCTV system picture monitors. Most TV receivers, however, are not designed for continuous duty (24 hours per day, every day) nor to the same standards as a professional-grade video monitor. When a TV receiver is used as a monitor, the input signal is a video-modulated RF signal obtained directly from a camera that produces both a video signal and an RF signal or from a TV modulator.

Two or more TV receivers may be fed by one video-modulator RF signal through splitters (couplers) as shown in Fig. 9. In this example, three two-way splitters are used. All of the TV receivers are set to receive on the same channel and all reproduce the same picture, but without sound.

TV MODULATORS

A TV modulator, such as the one shown in Fig. 10, is actually a low-power television broadcast transmitter. It generates two RF

Fig. 10. Catel TM-2300 television modulator. The channel frequencies are determined by the plug-in module at the right.

signals, one modulated by the video (picture) signal, the other modulated by the audio (sound) signal. Both RF signals are fed simultaneously to the input of one or more RF receivers. (When tuned to a TV broadcast station, a TV receiver intercepts two RF signals simultaneously, one representing the picture and the other representing the sound.) The carrier frequencies of these two RF

CLOSED CIRCUIT TELEVISION

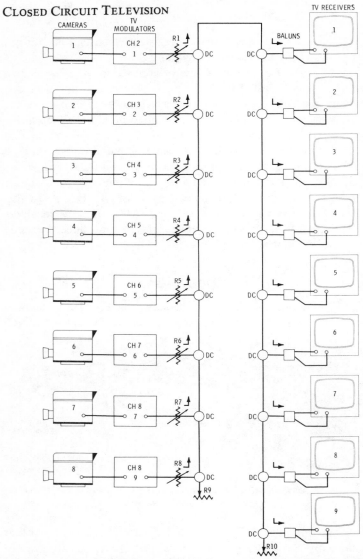

Fig. 11. Example of a CCTV system employing eight cameras, eight TV modulators and nine TV receivers as modulators. The RF outputs of the modulators are fed through variable attenuators (R1 through R8) to directional couplers to the TV receivers through directional couplers. R1 and R9 are 75-ohm terminators. The level of each RF channel can be adjusted individually with R1 through R8.

signals, whether received from a TV broadcast station or a professional TV modulator, are 4.5 MHz apart. In CCTV applications, the use of the sound channel is optional.

Up to 12 TV modulators may be used to feed picture signals (and sound signals when required) to one or more TV receivers. Each TV modulator is set to generate signals on different VHF TV channel frequencies (Channels 2 - 13). If each TV modulator is connected to a different camera, the picture picked up by any camera can be viewed at any of the associated TV receivers by appropriate setting of the receiver's channel selector.

Fig. 11 shows an example of a CCTV system employing eight cameras, eight TV modulators and eight TV receivers which enable simultaneous monitoring of all of the cameras. TV receiver

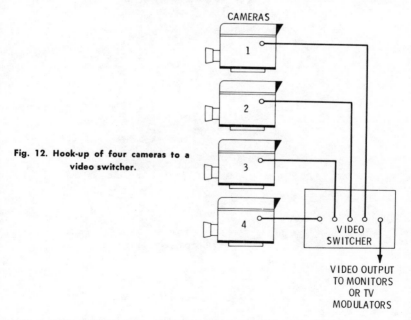

CAMERAS

Fig. 12. Hook-up of four cameras to a
video switcher.

VIDEO
SWITCHER

VIDEO OUTPUT
TO MONITORS
OR TV
MODULATORS

1 is tuned to receive from TV modulator 1, receiver 2 is tuned to receiver from modulator 2, and so on. The diagram also shows a ninth TV receiver which can be tuned to receive from any of the modulators as required. Additional TV receivers can be connected

197

to the system through splitters or directional couplers to provide more monitoring points.

VIDEO SWITCHERS

Whether camera outputs are fed as video signals to video monitors or to TV modulators which in turn feed RF signals to TV receivers, camera outputs can be first fed to a video switcher, as shown in Fig. 12. In this example, the video output of any of four cameras can be selected and fed to a video monitor or TV modulator. An example of a video switcher is shown in Fig. 13.

Courtesy GBC Electronics

Fig. 13. Example of a simple video switcher.

SYNC GENERATORS

As stated earlier, the built-in sync generator of a vidicon camera synchronizes the scanning of the camera and monitor (or

TV receiver when used as a monitor). When two or more cameras are used alternately to feed signals into the same system, the cameras are not in synchronism with each other. When switching from one camera to another, picture roll-over may result. This problem can be eliminated or at least minimized by employing an external sync generator (Fig. 14) to control all components of the system.

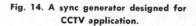

Fig. 14. A sync generator designed for CCTV application.

Courtesy Panasonic

The output of the sync generator is connected to the cameras directly or through the video mixer or a pulse distribution amplifier by means of coaxial cable.

CONTROL CENTERS

An example of a small-scale TV control center is shown in Fig. 15. It enables selection of cameras, production of video effects (image splitting, etc.), control of sound channels and other television station capabilities.

In a security system application, such a control center can be used for picking up pictures and sound from four locations. In addition, a videotape recorder can be connected to the control center, as shown in Fig. 16, to enable recording and play-back of information viewed by the cameras. The video output of the control center can be fed to external video monitors and/or to a TV modulator for further distribution.

199

Courtesy Concord Communications Systems

Fig. 15. Small-scale TV control center.

More complex TV control centers are available as standard items and custom built to meet unusual requirements.

LIGHTING

Using conventional cameras, high definition pictures require adequate illumination. Fluourescent lamps provide good illumination but low-contrast pictures. Incandescent spot and flood lamps provide high-intensity illumination. But, more TV experts prefer the use of quartz-halogen lamps which provide bright illumination and good picture quality because of their broad color temperature range.

Illumination of areas to be televised can be continuous. But, this can be expensive in terms of electric power cost. When lamps are remotely controlled, particularly from a considerable distance, heavy wiring is required in order to avoid excessive waste of power in the wires.

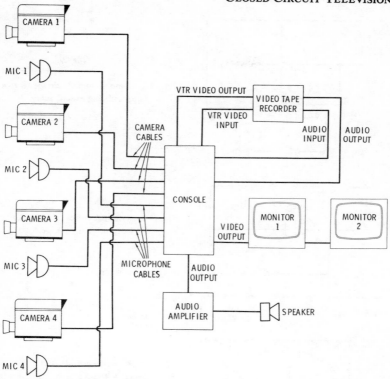

Fig. 16. A CCTV system utilizing four cameras, four microphones, a video tape recorder, an audio amplifier and speakers and two video monitors interconnected through a TV control center.

Lamps can be controlled by relays, triacs or a combination of relays and triacs through small-gage control circuits. Fig. 17 shows a lamp control circuit utilizing a 24-volt AC relay. The use of a triac as an electronic switch is depicted in Fig. 18. Closing the switch connects a resistor to the gate of the triac, causing it to conduct most of the time during each half-cycle of the AC supply voltage. To isolate the power line from the control circuit, both a transformer and triac can be used as shown in Fig. 19.

When a number of lights at various locations are to be controlled from a central location, the remote control scheme illustrated in Fig. 20 can be utilized.

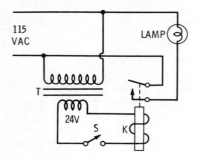

Fig. 17. Remote-control circuit for a lamp utilizing an AC relay.

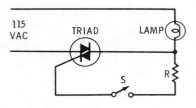

Fig. 18. Remote-control circuit for a lamp utilizing a triac.

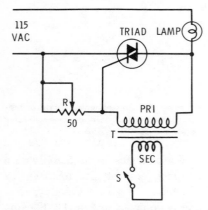

Fig 19. Remote-control circuit for a lamp using a triac and a transformer is used to isolate the switch from the power line.

RESIDENTIAL BUILDING PROTECTION

Tenants can view persons at the entrance of an apartment building on the screens of their television receivers when the building is equipped with an MATV (Master Antenna TeleVision) system. A television camera is placed where a good view of the entrance is obtained. The video output of the camera is fed to the video input of a TV modulator whose RF output in turn is fed into the MATV system for distribution to all of the TV antenna outlets in the building. As shown in Fig. 21, the RF signals from the TV modulator are inserted into the antenna system network through a combiner. The modulator is set to operate on a TV channel not in use in the area. For example, if channels 2 and 4 are received by the MATV system, the modulator could operate on Channel 3.

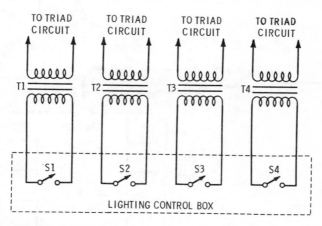

Fig. 20. Simplified circuit of a remote-control system for lamps at four camera locations by individual switches.

To enable hearing the conversations of persons seeking entrance to the building, a concealed microphone can be installed and connected to the audio input of the TV modulator through a preamplifier, as shown in Fig. 22. The preamplifier is required for boosting the output level of the microphone (typically -50 to -70 dB) to a power level of -10 dBm as required at the 600-ohm audio input of the modulator (such as the Catel TM-2200A). This aural surveillance feature is optional and should not be used where prohibited by law.

Normally, the MATV system head end equipment is installed in a shelter on the roof or on the top floor of the building near the antennas, particularly in high-rise buildings. The TV modulator can be installed near the camera in which case its RF output is

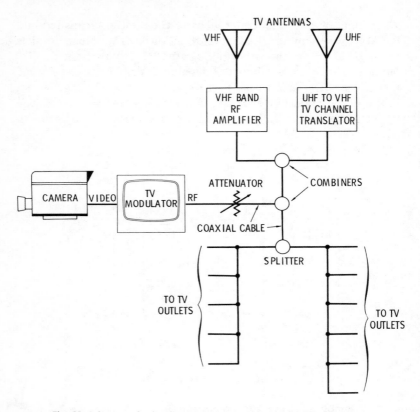

Fig. 21. Injection of a locally originated TV signal into an MATV system.

fed through a 75-ohm coaxial cable to the combiner. Or, the TV modulator can be installed adjacent to the head end equipment in which case the video output of the camera is fed through a 75-ohm coaxial cable to the modulator. If the aural surveillance feature is used, it will be necessary to also run a shielded twisted-pair cable from the preamplifier (near the microphone) to the audio input of the distant modulator, as shown in Fig. 23.

The camera and modulator can be left turned on at all times. When a visitor at the building entrance rings a tenant's bell to gain entrance into the building, the tenant sets the TV receiver to the closed-circuit channel to see who is at the door.

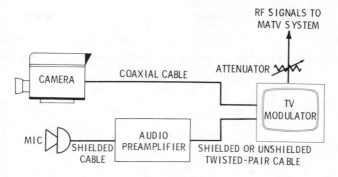

Fig. 22 Connections for both aural and visual signals fed to a TV modulator when it is located near the MATV head end.

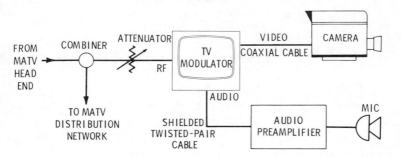

Fig. 23. Two long cables must be run to the TV modulator when it is located near the MATV head end.

In buildings which have a doorman or a security guard, cameras can be installed to view service garage, basement, and lobby floor elevator entrances. Since the video signals need not be distributed to the apartments, a video monitor can be provided for each camera, as shown in Fig. 24 or, as shown in Fig. 25, one video monitor can be used in conjunction with a coaxial switch or video switcher for selecting the video outputs of the cameras. All of the components are connected together through 75-ohm coaxial cable.

A camera can be concealed within an enclosure such as the one shown in Fig. 26. When a camera is to be installed at a location where there is a chance of its being stolen, it can be installed within a theftproof enclosure, such as the one shown in Fig. 27.

205

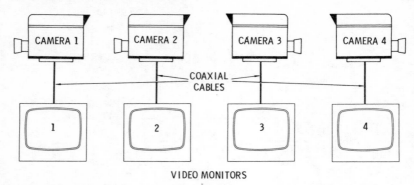

VIDEO MONITORS

Fig. 24. Four-camera CCTV system in which each camera is connected to its own monitor.

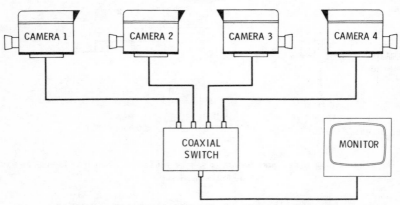

Fig 25. Four-camera CCTV system employing a single monitor and a camera selector.

LOW LIGHT LEVEL CAMERAS

Television cameras are available which can literally see in the dark. Fig. 28 shows two video monitors. The one at the left is connected to a conventional camera. The one at the right is connected to a low-light-level camera. Both cameras are focused on the same dimly lit scene. It can be noted that there is no picture on the screen at the left but that there is a picture on the screen at the right. An example of a low-light-level camera is shown in Fig. 29.

CAMERA CONTROL

In most security applications, cameras are permanently adjusted to view specific areas. A camera, however, can be installed on a remotely controlled pan-tilt platform. The camera shown in Fig. 30 can be controlled from a distance. A simplified diagram of a remote camera control system is shown in Fig. 31. Switches *S1*, *S2* and *S3* are of the three-position type. All are shown in the

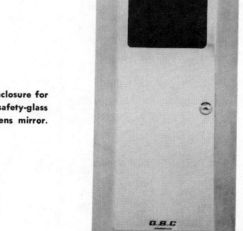

Fig. 26. Lobby or elevator enclosure for a TV camera. It has a safety-glass window and a wide-angle lens mirror.

Courtesy GBC Electronics

OFF position. When *S1* is set to the LEFT position, the motor causes the camera to pan to the left. When aimed in the desired horizontal direction, *S1* is set to the OFF position to stop the motor. To pan to the right, *S1* is set to the RIGHT position. When *S1* is set to the UP position, the camera is tilted upward, and in the DOWN position of *S2*, the camera is tilted downward. Switch *S3* is used for focusing the lens on distant or near objects in the same manner.

VIDEO RECORDERS

A videotape recorder (VTR) can be connected to a CCTV system to enable recording scenes of special interest. When a CCTV monitoring point is left unattended, the video output of a camera or video switcher can be fed to a VTR which will record what the camera sees until an attendant returns. The tape can then be played back to find out if anything unusual happened. If nothing of value had been recorded on the tape, it can be erased and used over again.

Courtesy GBC Electronics

Fig. 27. Theftproof TV camera enclosure.

The magnetic video disc recorder shown in Fig. 32 employs a removable, interchangeable disc. The removable *Discassette* cartridge uses flexible media which contains magnetic material on which picture information is recorded. The recorder slot loads in less than 10 seconds. The disc recorder system is essentially im-

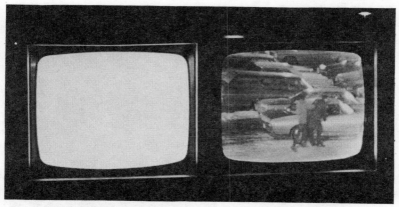

Fig. 28. Comparison of the sensitivity of a conventional TV camera connected to the left monitor. A low-light-level camera is connected to the right monitor.

Courtesy Motorola

Fig. 29. Low-light-level camera.

mune to vibration, and therefore suitable for use in most industrial environments.

The disc recorder can be used to make electronic slides, (still pictures of scenes seen by the camera). Each *Discassette* cartridge contains 300 fully interlaced, stable, full resolution still frames. The ability to rapidly change discs, and easily cue image sequences makes it easy to retrieve any scene. A 4′ file of *Discassette* cart-

Courtesy U.S. Navy

Fig. 30. The camera shown here can be focused, turned, and tilted from a remote location.

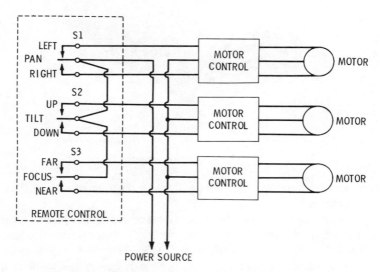

Fig. 31. Example of a circuitry of a remote-camera-control system.

210

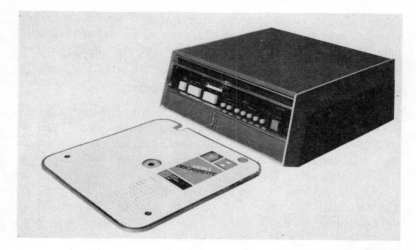

Fig. 32. Video disc recorder employing interchangeable Discassette cartridges.

Fig. 33. Weatherproof television camera.

211

ridges will store 10,000 full resolution frames. Push button record/ playback rates of 1, 3, 6, 10 or 15 frames per second are available, permitting selection of stop motion, slow motion or motion modes.

GENERAL CONSIDERATIONS

Since television cameras used in security systems must be dependable, only high-quality cameras should be selected. When installed out of doors or in a corrosive environment, the camera should be enclosed in a protective housing unless the camera is specifically designed for such use. (See Fig. 33).

To ensure long camera life and optimum performance, the camera should be operated at rated power input voltage. Where the AC supply voltage is high, low or subject to significant variations, the use of an AC line voltage regulator between the camera and the power line is recommended.

Monitors and other television system components should also be protected from environmental damage and power line voltage variations. A CCTV system should be designed by an expert but may be installed by a competent electrician or technician in accordance with the designer's or manufacturer's recommendations.

CHAPTER 9

Transmission Media

In a security system, both signals and power are transmitted. Signals can be transmitted through wires or coaxial cable or as radio-frequency energy transmitted through space or superimposed on power lines. Power, on the other hand, is transmitted only through metallic conductors. Although electric power is controlled by sensors, they are considered as signal transmitters. And, annunciators and other display devices are considered as signal receivers, although they consume at least a small amount of electric power.

Both signal and power transmission lines introduce "transmission losses" due to series resistance and also, in some cases, due to shunt resistances, shunt capacitance, and series inductance.

TRANSMISSION LINES FOR DC

The least amount of wire is required when an earth ground return path is used, as illustrated in Fig. 1. This technique was used in early Morse telegraph systems. In this example of a single wire, ground return circuit, battery B is connected to one end of the line and to an earth ground. A bell is connected to the other end of the line and also to an earth ground. The arrows indicate the direction of electron current flow. The current flows from the

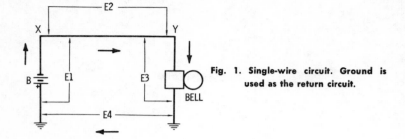

Fig. 1. Single-wire circuit. Ground is used as the return circuit.

negative battery terminal through the single wire line and the bell and back to the positive terminal of the battery through the ground. The voltage $E3$ across the bell is less than the voltage $E1$ across the battery because of the voltage drop $E2$ through the wire and the voltage drop $E4$ through the ground return path. Where the earth is moist and a good ground connection is made at each end of the circuit, the voltage drop $E4$ can be surprisingly small. Where the earth is dry, this voltage drop can be exorbitant. The voltage $E3$ across the bell is often subject to variations, not because of any significant variation in the wire line between points X and Y, but because of ground current which may either add to the voltage drop $E4$ or decrease this voltage drop, depending upon the polarity of the earth current.

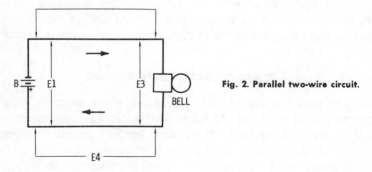

Fig. 2. Parallel two-wire circuit.

Much more reliable is the familiar two wire circuit shown in Fig. 2. Here the resistance of each of the lines must be considered.

214

If the battery delivers 6 volts *(E1)*, the bell resistance is 6-ohms and the resistance of each wire is 1-ohm, the loop resistance exclusive of the internal resistance of the battery is 8-ohms. Therefore, the current through the circuit is 0.75 ampere. The voltage drop *E2* is 0.75 volt as is the voltage drop *E4*. Therefore, the total voltage drop in the line is 1.5 volt and the voltage *E3* reaching the bell is only 4.5 volts. The transmission loss depends upon the length of the line and upon the diameter of the wires used. Table 1 lists the resistances of various sizes of copper wire.

Table 1. Wire Resistance

AWG	R/100 feet (ohms)	AWG	R/100 feet (ohms)
10	0.10	19	0.80
12	0.16	20	1.02
13	0.20	22	1.62
14	0.25	24	2.57
16	0.40	26	4.08
18	0.64	30	10.32

Instead of two parallel or twisted wires, single conductor shielded cable can be used to connect the battery to the bell as shown in Fig. 3. Here the transmission loss depends upon the

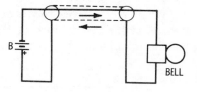

Fig. 3. Single-conductor shielded cable circuit.

diameter of the inner conductor of the cable and upon the resistance of the cable shield. In this circuit, the shield serves as the return electric current path.

When more than one load is connected across a transmission line, the transmission losses will be greater. Fig. 4 shows two bells connected across a two-wire line. The voltage *E2* at bell 1 will be higher than the voltage *E3* across bell 2. Assume that the battery *B*

215

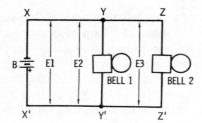

Fig. 4. Two loads on the same circuit.

delivers 6 volts *(E1)* and that each bell has a resistance of 6 ohms. If the resistance of the line from point X to point Z is 1-ohm and the resistance of the other line from point X' to Z' is also 1-ohm, the total line resistance will be 2-ohms. If bell 1 were not connected across the line, the current through the circuit would be 0.75 ampere and the voltage $E3$ across bell 2 would be 4.5 volts. However, with bell 1 connected across the line at points Y and Y', the voltage drop between point X and point Y and between point X' and point Y' will be increased. The voltage drop between the battery and bell 1 will be approximately 1.4 volts. This means that $E2$ will be 4.6 volts. There will be an additional voltage drop between bell 1 and bell 2 of approximately 0.65 volts. Therefore, $E3$ will be approximately 3.95 volts.

OPEN CIRCUIT TRANSMISSION LINES

When NO sensors are connected in parallel across a single transmission line as, shown in Fig. 5, the current through the bell will be minimum when sensor *S1* is closed and maximum when

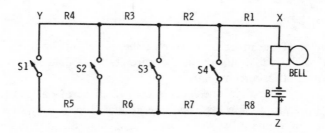

Fig. 5. Open-circuit sensors paralleled across same line.

sensor *S4* is closed because of the longer current path through *S1*. In this diagram, *R1* and *R8* represent the line resistance between bell and battery and sensor *S4*; *R2* and *R7* represent the line resistance between *S4* and *S3*; *R3* and *R6* represent the line resistance between *S3* and *S2*; and *R4* and *R5* represent the line resistance between *S2* and *S1*. The reliability of the system depends upon the overall loop resistance from point *X* through *Y* and back to *Z*.

Another way of connecting NO sensors in parallel is shown in Fig. 6. Here, instead of being bridged across a single parallel line, a separate pair of wires is run to each of the sensors. Whether to use the circuit shown in Fig. 5 or the one shown in Fig. 6,

Fig. 6. Open-circuit sensors on separate lines.

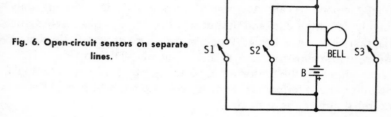

depends upon the layout of the building and the overall amount of wire required.

CLOSED CIRCUIT TRANSMISSION LINES

Fig. 7 is a schematic presentation of a closed circuit alarm system employing 4 NC sensors *(S1, S2, S3, S4)*. In this kind of

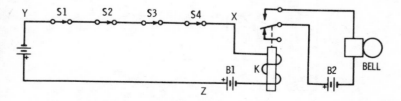

Fig. 7. Closed-circuit sensors in series on same line.

circuit, the loop resistance *(X-Y-Z)* is always the same as long as the sensor contacts are closed. When the loop distance is considerable, a relay which requires less current than the bell is used as shown in the diagram.

ANALOG SIGNAL TRANSMISSION LINES

An NO or NC sensor transmits a digital signal. It has only two states, ON or OFF. An analog sensor, such as a thermistor or a strain gauge bridge, on the other hand, transmits analog information. The frequency of the signal it transmits may be so low that it can be treated as a purely DC signal. Depending upon the frequency of the physical change detected by the sensor, the frequency of the resulting signal can be fairly high. Then, the signal must be looked upon as an AC signal even if it is DC varying only slightly in amplitude and frequency. Fig. 8 is a block schematic diagram showing a bridge type transducer connected through a two-wire transmission line to the input of a DC amplifier. If the signal output of the sensor is very low, the transmission line might pick up noise interference and/or radio signals which could affect the reliability of the system.

Inductive pickup of interference can be reduced by using twisted pair cable as shown in Fig. 9A. Immunity from electrostatic pickup of interference can be achieved by using a cable consisting of a twisted pair covered by a shield as shown in Fig. 9B. The shield can be grounded at one end as shown in the diagram.

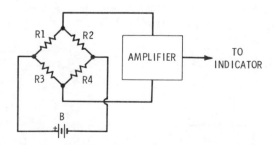

Fig. 8. Bridge-type sensor connected to DC amplifier through two-wire parallel line.

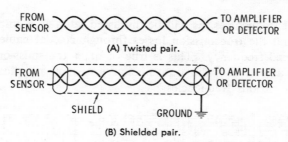

(A) Twisted pair.

(B) Shielded pair.

Fig. 9. Noise-reduction transmission lines.

More widely used is coaxial cable. A coaxial cable is actually a concentric cable which has a single inner conductor surrounded by insulation which is covered by a solid or braided metal shield. The shield is usually, in turn, covered by a protective jacket. The difference between conventional single conductor shield cable and coaxial cable is the precision of manufacturing tolerances and design. Coaxial cable may be used as a substitute for conventional single conductor shielded cable. However, when used at its maximum capability, coaxial cable is used to interconnect devices whose impedance is the same as the characteristic impedance of the cable. The characteristic impedance of coaxial cable depends upon the diameter of the inner conductor, the spacing between the inner conductor and outer conductor (shield), and the type of insulation (dielectric) surrounding the inner conductor. When the impedance of the sensor and the impedance of the amplifier or detector to which it is connected is the same as the characteristic impedance of the cable, the shield of the cable may be grounded at both ends of the circuit as shown in Fig. 10.

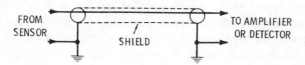

Fig. 10. Coaxial transmission line.

Coaxial cable offers considerable flexibility in security systems since it can be used for transmission of signals over a very wide range of frequencies, as will be discussed later. It is important to know that the transmission losses through coaxial cable increase with signal frequency. (This is true of other transmission lines as well.) Table 2 lists the transmission losses of a typical coaxial cable at various frequencies.

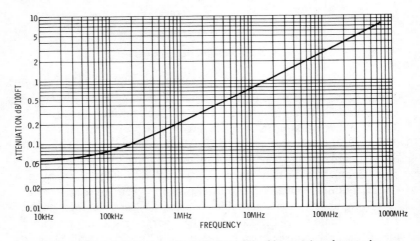

Table 2. Transmission losses of a typical coaxial cable at various frequencies.

CARRIER CURRENT TRANSMISSION

As previously discussed in Chapter 7, radio frequency signals can be transmitted over electric lines without affecting the other devices served by the power line. An example of an alarm system employing power line carrier current techniques is shown in Fig. 11. The device at the lower right of the illustration is a remote signal transmitter which is plugged into an electric power outlet. The device plugged into the left side of the alarm device is a receiver which is actuated by the remote signal transmitter. When the remote signal transmitter is actuated by pushing a button or by a sensor, a radio signal is transmitted through the power line to the receiver at the alarm control unit.

In a typical home, electric power is distributed from a three wire circuit as illustrated in Fig. 12. Of the three wires (X Y Z), Y

Fig. 11. Crime alert system that is actuated by a plug-in radio transmitter.

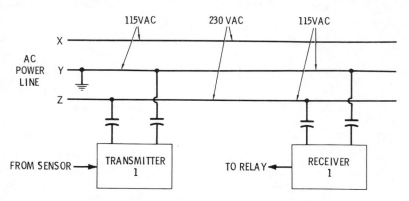

Fig. 12. Example of power-line-carrier signal transmission circuit.

is connected to an earth ground. Although the voltage across X and Z is around 230 volts, the voltage between X and ground and between Z and ground is in the order of 115 volts. This three-wire circuit makes it possible to feed 230 volts to electric ranges, air conditioners, and other heavy duty appliances and 115 volts to wall outlets and lamps.

In a power line carrier system, the RF signals generated by a transmitter are capacitively coupled to the power line, as shown in Fig. 12. The receiver is also connected to the power line in the same manner. In a control system application, the sensor is connected to the transmitter and the output of the receiver is connected to a relay which activates an alarm or other display device. Several transmitters and receivers may be connected to the same power line without mutual interference if each derived circuit operates at different radio frequency.

TONE MULTIPLEXING

The transmitter previously shown in Fig. 12 can be turned on and off by the sensor and the receiver can simply sense the presence or absence of a radio signal. In a more sophisticated system, the transmitter is modulated by one or more tone transmitters. A simple block diagram of a 4-channel signalling system is given in Fig. 13. Here, the radio transmitter *(TX)* is modulated by tone

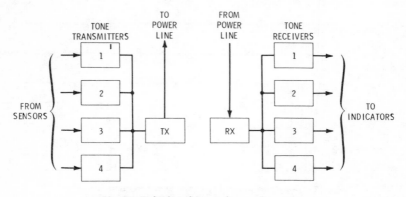

Fig. 13. Multiplexed power-line-carrier system.

transmitters, each of which operates at a different frequency within the audio spectrum. The radio signal, modulated by one or more of the tone signals, is fed to the power line. The receiver intercepts these signals and feeds them to tone receivers, each receptive to a tone signal at a specific frequency. This technique for transmitting two or more signal channels simultaneously over the same transmission medium is known as tone multiplexing.

A simplified block diagram of an ON-OFF tone channel is given in Fig. 14. The tone transmitter is turned ON and OFF by

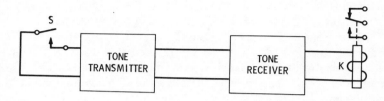

Fig. 14. On-off tone signaling channel.

sensor S. The tone receiver is turned so that it will respond only to a signal at the same frequency as that generated by the tone transmitter. When S is closed and a tone signal is transmitted to the receiver, the audio frequency tone is rectified and converted into a DC signal which is amplified and energizes a relay. The contacts of the relay can be used to actuate an alarm or display device. A more widely used tone signaling technique is illustrated in Fig. 15. Instead of the sensor turning the tone transmitter on and off, the sensor causes the tone transmitter to shift its frequency. This is

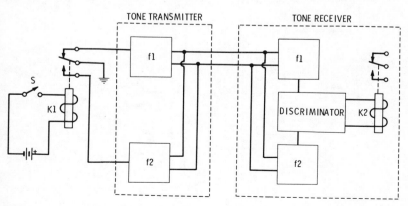

Fig. 15. FSK tone signaling channel.

known as FSK which stands for *frequency-shift keying*. Referring to the diagram, assume that the oscillator within the tone transmitter that operates on frequency *f1* is normally operational and that the oscillator operating on *f2* is normally nonoperational. Normally, the receiver intercepts *f1*. It is the normal presence of a signal on *f1* that indicates that the system is operational.

When sensor *S* is closed, relay *K* is energized causing the *f1* oscillator to stop and to turn on the *f2* oscillator. Now, the signal intercepted by the tone receiver is at *f2* instead of *f1*. The discriminator within the tone receiver senses this change of frequency and energizes relay *K2*.

This diagram is symbolic of what happens. In actual equipment, the transition from *f1* to *f2* may be accomplished by changing the frequency of a single oscillator. Likewise, the tone receiver can be receptive to either *f1* or *f2* and determination of which is being received is the function of the discriminator. The advantage of FSK tone signaling over on-off signaling is that there is always

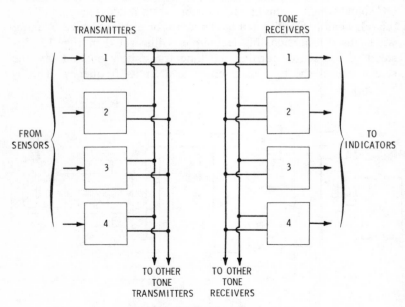

Fig. 16. Tone multiplex system.

a signal being transmitted. In an on-off tone system, this monitoring feature is not available.

The frequency determining devices in tone transmitters and tone receivers may be L-C (inductance-capacitance) or R-C (resistance-capacitance) filters or electro-mechanical resonators.

As previously shown in Fig. 13, a single line block diagram, tone channels can be stacked at both the radio transmitter and radio receiver. The same techniques can be applied to wire line transmission. Fig. 14, for the sake of simple explanation, the tone transmitter and tone receiver are interconnected through a pair of wires. The same is true in Fig. 15. A large number of tone channels may be transmitted over a single pair of wires, as illustrated in Fig. 16. The interconnecting wires may be a parallel pair, twisted pair, shielded twisted pair or other two-wire circuit. Since the tone transmitters and tone receivers operate at different frequencies, it is possible to transmit a number of tones simultaneously without interference between tone channels. In the system shown in Fig. 16, tone receiver 1 responds only to the signal from tone transmitter 1 and so on.

The same pair of wires can be used for transmission of tones in both directions. As shown in Fig. 17, a tone signal can be transmitted in one direction at frequency *f1* and in the opposite direction at frequency *f2* without mutual interference. A number of tone

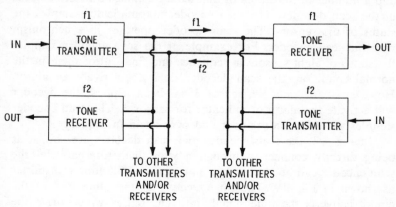

Fig. 17. Bidirectional tone signaling system.

transmitters and receivers can be connected in the same fashion across the same line to provide a number of tone channels in both directions.

ELECTRONIC SCANNERS

When a number of tone transmitters and receivers are used as previously discussed, the multiplexing technique is known as *frequency division multiplexing* (FDM). In most security system applications, it is not necessary to transmit all signals at the same time as when FDM is used. Instead, the transmission medium may be shared by a number of circuits by employing *time divison multplexing* (TDM). A simple example is shown in Fig. 18. Here a scan

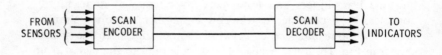

Fig. 18. Electronic scanning system utilizing DC pulse transmission.

encoder is connected through a wire line to a scan decoder. A number of sensors are connected to the input of the scan encoder and a number of indicators or alarms are connected to the outputs of the scan decoder. The scan encoder automatically samples the status of the sensors. The scan decoder operates in synchronism with the scan encoder. For example, if the scan encoder samples the status of eight sensors in sequence and finds all of them in the normal condition, the scan decoder does not activate an alarm. However, if for example, sensor 3 has been tripped, the decoder will activate the alarm or indicator for sensor 3. The scan encoder samples all of its sensors over and over again in sequence.

In Fig. 18, the scan encoder and scan decoder are shown as being directly connected through a wire line. Alternatively, the scan encoder can be used to key an on-off or FSK tone transmitter as shown in Fig. 19. The tone receiver at the other end of the circuit converts the tone signals into DC pulses which drive the scan decoder.

When a large number of sensors must be sensed, several scan encoders and scan decoders can be used, each interconnected through a tone channel operating at a different frequency.

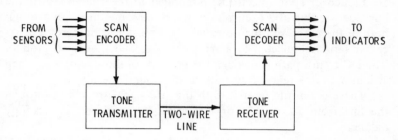

Fig. 19. Block diagram of a tone channel employing electronic scanning.

VOICE-PLUS-SIGNAL CIRCUITS

A DC control or alarm circuit can be superimposed upon an AC or audio frequency transmission circuit, as illustrated in Fig. 20. The transmission line can be used for conveying AC electric power from X to Y or Y to X, or for transmitting audio frequency signals from an amplifier whose output is fed to the primary of

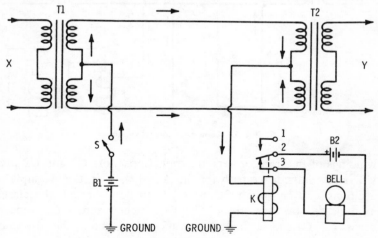

Fig. 20. Simplexed-to-ground control circuit.

227

transformer *T1* (at point *X*) to another transformer *(T2)* at point *Y* to a loudspeaker connected to the secondary of *T2*. Or, this could be a telephone or intercom line. The line side winding of *T1* and *T2* are tapped or split. When DC is applied to the center tap of the line side winding of *T1,* current flows in the same direction through both of the wires and then through the line side winding of *T2*. Its center tap is connected to a relay winding and thence to ground. The DC return path is through the ground. In this example, closing switch *S* causes relay *K* to pull in and sound the alarm.

There is no interference with the AC signal travelling through the line from *T1* to *T2* or vice-versa if the circuit is carefully balanced.

Another way of transmitting DC through a circuit used for AC or audio frequency transmission is shown in Fig. 21. The line side

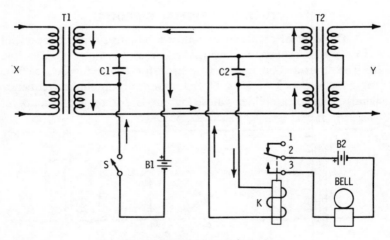

Fig. 21. Composite control circuit.

windings of the transformers are split. Capacitors *C1* and *C2* provide a low impedance path for the AC signals. In this example of a circuit, closing switch *S* causes DC to flow through the circuit as indicated by the arrows. The DC applied across *C1* appears across *C2*. Of course, there is a voltage drop due to the resistance of the transformer windings and the transmission line.

228

VOICE FREQUENCY MULTIPLEXING

Normally, only one voice frequency conversation can be conducted over a single pair of wires. However, three talking circuits can be transmitted over two pairs of wires as illustrated in Fig. 22.

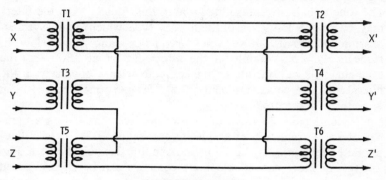

Fig. 22. Phantom circuit.

This is known as a phantom circuit. The third channel is derived by connecting transformer $T3$ to the center taps of the line side windings of transformers $T1$ and $T5$ and by connecting $T4$ to the center taps of the line side windings of $T2$ and $T6$. Voice and/or

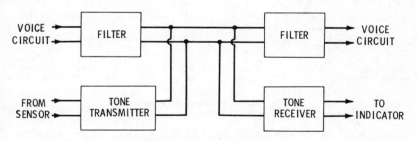

Fig. 23. Voice-plus-tone circuit.

tone signals can be transmitted from X to X', or in the opposite direction, from Y to Y' or in the opposite direction or from Z to Z' or in the opposite direction with very little cross-talk if all of the circuits are carefully balanced.

229

One or more tone channels can be transmitted over a voice circuit wire line. As shown in Fig. 23, a filter is used at each end of the circuit to remove the tone signals from the talking circuit. These filters may be "notch" filters which stop transmission of signals within a narrow band within the voice frequency range. The tone signals are transmitted within this "notch." Or, the filters may be of the low pass or high pass type which enables transmission of signals above voice frequency range, or below it, respectively. For example, if the filters cut off at 2800 Hz, the tone channels can operate at higher frequencies. Conversely, if the filters cut off frequencies below 300 Hz, the tone channels can operate at lower frequencies.

A single pair of wires can be used for accommodating a number of voice frequency channels by employing FDM carrier telephone equipment. As shown in the simplified block diagram Fig. 24, two or more carrier telephone channels can be superimposed

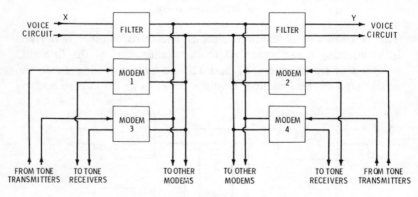

Fig. 24. Carrier telephone system.

on a physical telephone channel. Voice frequency signals are conveyed in either direction from X to Y through filters. These filters pass frequencies below approximately 3000 Hz and block the entry of signals of higher frequencies from the telephone or other devices connected at points X and Y. Parallel across the line are modems at each end of the circuit. Each modem consists of a low power radio frequency transmitter and radio frequency receiver.

230

Modem 1 transmits to modem 2 on frequency f1. Modem 2 transmits back to modem 1 on frequency f2. Similarly, modem 3 transmits to modem 4 on f3 and modem 4 transmits back to modem 3 on f4. The modems can be used for two-way transmission of voice signals or for transmission of multiplexed tone signals. Each modem can handle approximately 17 tone channels in each direction, depending upon the type of tone equipment used and the speed at which the tone transmitters are keyed.

COAXIAL CABLE TRANSMISSION SYSTEMS

Coaxial cable can be used for transmitting signals at frequencies ranging from DC to several hundred megahertz. In CATV (cable television) systems, for example, coaxial cable is used for transmission of twelve or more television channels simultaneously. In a security system application, coaxial cable can be used as the transmission medium for both alarm signals and television pictures. An example of such a system is shown in Fig. 25. The RF output

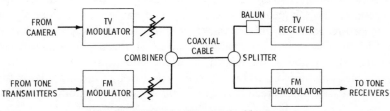

Fig. 25. Video-plus-FM coaxial cable circuit.

of a TV modulator is fed through an attenuator to a signal combiner. Also, an RF signal from an FM modulator is fed through another attenuator to the same combiner. The combined RF signals are fed through coaxial cable to a splitter. In this example, one output port of the splitter is fed through a balun to a TV receiver for reproducing the television picture that was generated by a television camera whose output was fed to the input of TV modulator. The other output port of the splitter is fed to an FM demodulator. The FM channel can be used for transmission of a number of tone channels in much the same manner as over a pair of wires or a radio link.

A coaxial cable can be tapped at any point for dropping and inserting signals. Fig. 26 shows an example of a security applica-

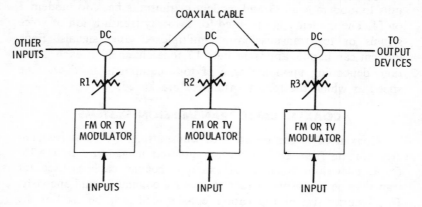

Fig. 26. Multiple-input coaxial cable system.

tion, wherein signals are injected into the line. A directional coupler (DC) is inserted into the coaxial cable line at each signal insertion point. In this example, it is shown that signals from an FM or TV modulator can be inserted at three points along the line. When a TV modulator is used, television signals from a camera can be fed into the coaxial cable through the modulator for transmission at differing frequencies. When FM modulators are used, they can be modulated by one or more tone transmitters. At the receiving end of the circuit (not shown) a separate demodulator is provided for each of the modulators.

The capacity of a coaxial cable transmission line is so great that it can be used for transmission of hundreds of unidirectional or bidirectional voice frequency carrier channels, each of which

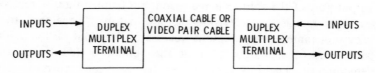

Fig. 27. Multichannel telephone carrier system utilizing coaxial or video-pair cable as the transmission medium.

232

can be modulated by voice signals or a number of tone signals. Fig. 27 is a simplified block diagram of a high density coaxial cable transmission system.

RADIO LINKS

Alarm or control signals can be transmitted in the form of tones over a radio link. As shown in Fig. 28, radio signals are

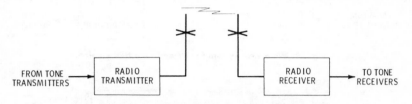

Fig. 28. Radio link for tone transmission.

transmitted through space from the radio transmitter to the radio receiver. The radio transmitter can be modulated by one or more tone transmitters and the output of the radio receiver can be fed to one or more tone receivers. Each tone channel can be used as an independent alarm or control circuit. When used with an electronic scanner as previously described, each tone channel can be used for conveying numerous alarm or control signals.

For short distance transmission, the radio transmitter and radio receiver may operate within the 160-190 kHz, 540-1600 kHz or 26.96-27.26 MHz bands without a radio station license being required, provided the transmitter power and antenna length are limited as prescribed in Part 15, FCC Rules and Regulations.

For inter-plant communications, such a system operated within the 72-76 MHz band in areas not served by television broadcast station operating on either or both channels 4 and/or 5. On this band, transmission over considerable distances (up to 50 miles or so) is possible. Relatively long haul transmission is also permitted on the frequencies 27.235, 27.245, 27.255, 27.265 and 27.275 MHz when covered by an appropriate station license. On these specific frequencies, it is permissible to transmit voice or any other

233

kind of information as long as the band occupancy of the radio signal does not exceed 8 kHz.

Microwave links may be used for transmission of alarm and control signals as well as television under an appropriate radio

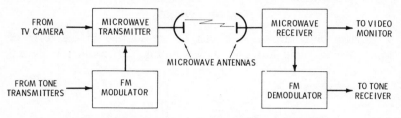

Fig. 29. Microwave system for TV and tone transmission.

Courtesy Jerrold Electronics Corp.

Fig. 30. Typical microwave transmission.

station license. A block diagram of an example of a microwave radio link for simultaneous television and control/alarm signal transmission is depicted in Fig. 29. The video signal from the camera is fed directly (or through a video switcher) to the microwave transmitter. The tone signals are fed to the output of an FM modulator whose RF output is fed to a microwave transmitter, such as the one shown in Fig. 30. At the other end of the system, the FM signal is fed to an FM demodulator whose output is fed to tone receivers. The video output of the receiver is fed to a video monitor or video signal distribution system. As Fig. 29 indicates, parabolic antennas are used for transmitting the signal from one station to the other. These antennas, which are similar to spot lights, transmit a narrow beam signal.

For satisfactory microwave transmission, a line-of-sight path is usually required. When objects intervene in the path between the transmitting antenna and the receiving antenna, a passive reflector can often be used to route the signal around the obstruction as in Fig. 31. The passive reflector is relatively large flat or concave

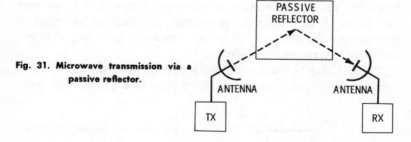

Fig. 31. Microwave transmission via a passive reflector.

metal surface which acts as a mirror for the microwave radio signals. An alternative type of passive repeater is depicted in Fig. 32. Here, the signals are intercepted by a parabolic antenna which is connected through wave guide or coaxial cable to another parabolic antenna which re-transmits to the receiving station.

When the distance between transmitting and receiving microwave stations exceed 15 miles or so or when propagation conditions make it impractical to use a passive repeater, an active repeater may be used. Fig. 33 is a simple block diagram of a

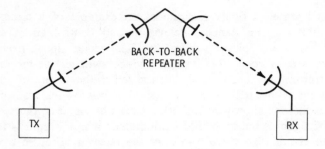

Fig. 32. Microwave transmission via a back-to-back passive repeater.

Fig. 33. Active, back-to-back microwave repeater.

back-to-back repeater consisting of a microwave receiver and a microwave transmitter. The receiving antenna intercepts signals on frequency $f1$ and the transmitting antenna re-transmits on frequency $f2$. It is necessary to transpose frequencies to prevent the output of the transmitter from being fed back to the input of the receiver. In the case of passive repeaters, however, it is not necessary to transpose frequencies.

Signals may be transmitted from one microwave transmitter to several microwave receivers, as illustrated in Fig. 34. This tech-

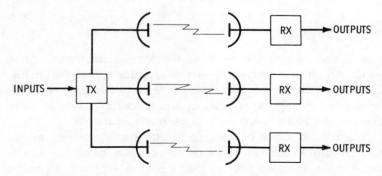

Fig. 34. Simplified example of an airlink microwave distribution system.

nique is utilized in airlink system developed by *Laser Link Corporation* for simultaneous transmission of a number of television programs from a central point to a number of cable television distribution points. In a security application, a number of CCTV and status signals could be transmitted from one point to two or more receiving locations. The intelligence carrying capacity of the airlink system is phenomenal. It is capable of handling thousands of alarm/control signals and/or several television channels.

When it is necessary to transmit television and/or a large number of control/alarm signals in both directions simultaneously, a duplex microwave system can be installed. Fig. 35 is a simplified

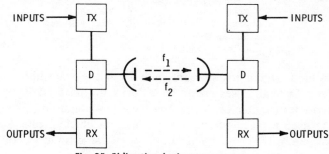

Fig. 35. Bidirectional microwave system.

block diagram of a single hop duplex microwave system. The transmitter at the left generates a signal on frequency *f1* which is fed through an antenna duplexer (*D*) to an antenna which is used for simultaneous transmission and reception. The *f1* signals are intercepted by the microwave station at the right and are fed through the duplexer to the receiver. Simultaneously, the transmitter at the right transmits through the duplexer on frequency *f2* to the receiver at the left. As in the case of a one-way microwave system, both television and control/alarm signals can be transmitted.

Microwave systems operate at frequencies above 900 MHz. Since the radio waves at these frequencies have properties similar to those of light, they can be transmitted as beams by using highly directional antennas. The limitations placed on the use of microwave transmission systems for security purposes are detailed in

Volume V, FCC Rules and Regulations which is available from the Superintendent of Documents, U.S. Government Printing Office, Washington, D.C. 20402.

OPTICAL COMMUNICATION LINKS

No license is required for transmission of signals over an infrared light beam. Transmission distance is limited to a few miles and is subject to deterioration by smoke, clouds and precipitation. As shown in Fig. 36, an invisible infrared light beam is

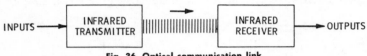

INPUTS → INFRARED TRANSMITTER ||||||||||||||||||||||||| INFRARED RECEIVER → OUTPUTS

Fig. 36. Optical communication link.

transmitted over a line-of-sight path from the transmitter to the receiver. Optical lenses are used to focus the infrared light beam from the transmitter to the receiver. Such a communications link can be used to accommodate one television channel plus a number of control/alarm signals or a very large number of control/alarm signals.

COMMON CARRIER FACILITIES

Telephone-grade circuits can be leased from telephone companies for interplant transmission of control/alarm signals. Each such voice grade circuit can be multiplexed to accommodate a number of tone channels. In some areas, so-called metallic circuits are also available for transmission of DC alarm and control signals. However, telephone companies are getting more reluctant about making such circuits available since the same pair of wires can be used for conveying more intelligence and commanding more revenue. In addition, video pair circuits are available from many telephone companies for transmission of television signals. In some communities, CATV companies can furnish radio or alarm circuits which are piggybacked on their cable television transmission facilities.

CHAPTER 10

Security
System Installation

The protection of a security system is no more secure than the manner in which it is installed and the reliability of its components. If the system components are connected together through wires that are readily accessible to intruders and if interconnections are hay-wire splices, the level of security is low.

RELIABILITY OF COMPONENTS

Electrical and electronic devices are rated in terms of MTBF (mean time before failure), expressed in hours, and under specified conditions. For example, a switch designed for operation within the 0 - 100° F range may be unreliable at −20° or 130° F and therefore should not be used out of doors or where such temperature extremes are apt to be encountered. Similarly, a device designed for use in a home may not be adequately reliable on board a boat or in an industrial plant.

The life of a component employing moving parts is affected both by time and the number of times it is operated, as well as by the environment in which it is used. While initial cost can be minimized by buying inexpensive components, maintenance costs can be considerably higher and the level of security can be low.

COMPONENT INTERCONNECTIONS

Fig. 1 shows how the components of an inexpensive AC-powered home security alarm system are connected together. The

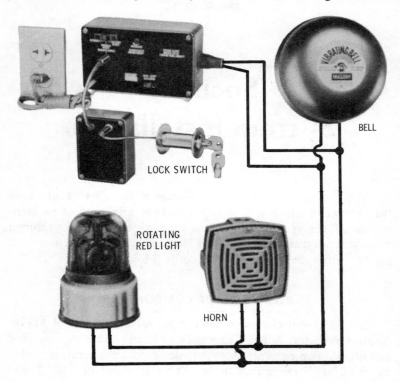

BELL

LOCK SWITCH

ROTATING
RED LIGHT

HORN

Courtesy P.R. Mallory and Co.

Fig. 1. Wiring requirements of a power-line-operated security alarm system.

wires can be run along baseboards, under the floor, etc. since they are not required to handle a significant amount of electric current. The wiring requirements of a similar system, operable from batteries, are illustrated in Fig. 2.

Many install-it-yourself security alarm kits include wire, usually two-wire parallel or twisted-pair wires which can be stapled or

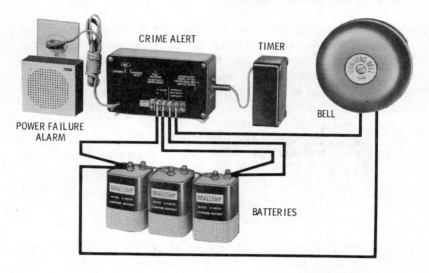

Fig. 2. Wiring requirements for a security alarm system employing batteries.

clamped to a flat surface. Such wire is usually adequate for the intended purpose. But, professionally-installed security system components are often interconnected by wires run through conduit, armored cable or other high-grade wires and cables.

TERMINAL BLOCKS

Although NO sensors can be attached to two-wire zip cord or similar wire through splices, and NC sensors can be inserted in

Fig. 3. Barrier terminal block.

241

series with one leg of a two-wire cable, the use of barrier terminal blocks at each location will result in a more professional and more reliable installation. A typical barrier terminal block is shown in Fig. 3. The looped ends of wires can be secured by the screws. Better, however, is to install crimp-on or soldered lugs to the end of each wire. The spade or hook lug is then held secure by a screw.

Fig. 4. Single-screw barrier terminal block.

Courtesy Minnesota Mining and Mfg. Co.

Another type of barrier terminal block, shown in Fig. 4, has only one screw per circuit. However, this type of terminal block is very flexible. As illustrated in Fig. 5, wires can be run through unbroken and without the insulation removed; contact is made when the screw is tightened. Insulated wires can also be terminated by pushing their ends under a screwhead and then tightening the screw. And, of course, wires with lugs can be accommodated.

Another type of terminal block into which wires, equipped with special lugs, are plugged in is shown in Fig. 6.

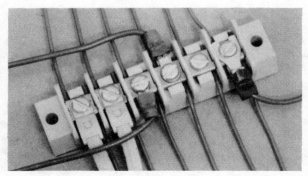

Courtesy Minnesota Mining and Mfg. Co.

Fig. 5. Scotchflex brand barrier terminal block showing how wires may be connected directly without stripping of insulation or by using lugs.

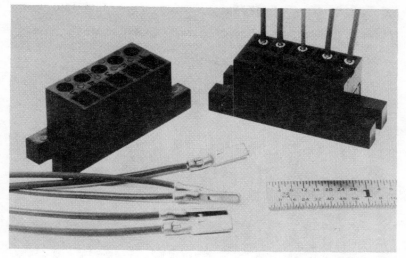

Courtesy Busstrip Co.

Fig. 6. Terminal block which accepts lug-equipped wires on a plug-in basis.

SPLICERS AND LUGS

At locations where sensors or other devices are not to be tapped into or bridged across a line, wires that need to be extended can be spliced in the conventional manner. More convenient, however, is to use solderless wire splicers, such as those shown in Fig. 7.

Because of the scarcity of copper, aluminum wire is often used in lieu of copper wire. Since it is difficult to solder lugs to the ends of aluminum wire, compression type lugs, such as those shown in Fig. 8, have been developed. They can be used with either aluminum or copper wires.

SPECIAL CABLES

In addition to round multiconductor cables and conventional flat two-wire electric power cables, special-purpose flat cables can be used for interconnecting security system components. These include television antenna twin-lead transmission line (often known as ribbon cable) which is available with various gauge conductors

243

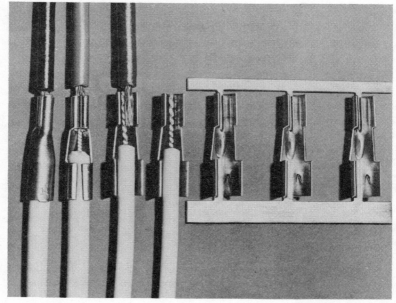

Courtesy Berg Mfg. Co.

Fig. 7. Solderless wire splices.

COMPRESSION TERMINAL LUGS

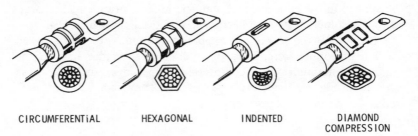

CIRCUMFERENTiAL HEXAGONAL INDENTED DIAMOND COMPRESSION

Fig. 8. Compression-type lugs for copper or aluminum wire.

and four- or five-conductor television antenna rotator cable. A flat electrical cable, available with various numbers of conductors, is shown in Fig. 9. Because it is flat, it can be run across floors, around doorways, etc.

Courtesy Minnesota Mining and Mfg. Co.

Fig. 9. Flat cable for installation across floors and doorways.

Where noise and/or radio signal pickup is a problem, shielded twisted-pair cable, video pair cable or shielded TV antenna twin-lead can be used. Shielded twin-lead cable has two parallel inner conductors for signal transmission surrounded by a braided shield, plus a "drain" wire for more adequate grounding of the shield.

Wires and cable that are exposed can be readily cut by an intruder. This possibility can be avoided by running the wires through metal conduit. Fig. 10 shows an example of the use of conduit for protecting the wires used to interconnect to outdoor-mounted equipment enclosures.

SENSOR LOCATION CONNECTIONS

In a professional-caliber installation, the connections to a sensor can be made through a barrier terminal block, mounted exposed where it can't be reached without a ladder, or enclosed in a metal box. Fig. 11 shows the connections at a barrier terminal block

245

Fig. 10. Example of conduit wiring to locked equipment housing.

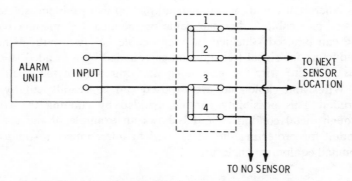

Fig. 11. Use of barrier terminal block at an open-circuit sensor location.

at or near a sensor location. Terminals 1 and 2 are connected together by jumper straps designed for use with terminal blocks of this type. Terminals 3 and 4 are connected together in the same manner.

246

Similar techniques can be employed when utilizing single conductor shielded cable as the transmission medium. As shown in Fig. 12, terminals 1 and 2 are strapped together and terminals 3

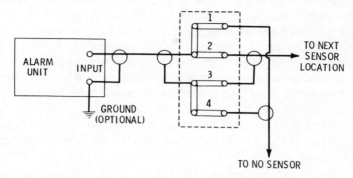

Fig. 12. Connections at barrier terminal block at an open-circuit sensor location when single conductors shielded cable is used.

and 4 of the terminal block are strapped together. The inner conductor of the cable is connected to terminal 2 and the shield to terminal 3. The inner conductor of the branch line shielded cable is connected to terminal 1 and its shield is connected to terminal 4.

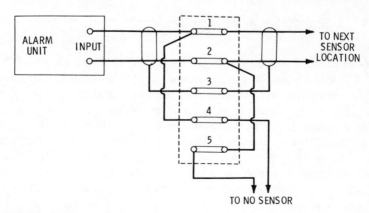

Fig. 13. Connections at barrier terminal block at an open-circuit sensor location when shielded twisted-pair cable is used.

247

The wiring arrangements used at a sensor location terminal block when shielded twisted pair cable is used are shown in Fig. 13. The two inner conductors of the line leading to the alarm unit are connected to terminals 1 and 2 and the line continuing on to the next central location is connected to the same terminals as shown. The shield of the incoming and the shield of the outgoing main line are connected together through terminal 3. Terminal 1 is connected to terminal 4 through a jumper wire and terminal 2 is connected to terminal 5 through another jumper wire. The shielded or unshielded pair of wires running to the NO sensor are connected to terminals 4 and 5.

The use of terminal blocks which have only two terminals is illustrated in Fig. 14. Here the line from the alarm unit is connected

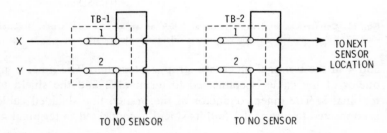

Fig. 14. Connections at open-circuit sensor locations where two-terminal barrier blocks are used.

to terminals 1 and 2 of *TB 1* and extended to terminals 1 and 2 of *TB 2* and so on. At each terminal block, the branch line to the NO sensor is also connected to terminals 1 and 2 as shown.

The wiring connections at terminal blocks to which NC sensors are connected can be as shown in Fig. 15. Here, the line from the alarm unit is connected to terminals 1 and 2 of *TB 1*. Terminal 2 is strapped to terminal 3 and the branch line to the NC sensor is connected to terminals 3 and 4. Terminals 1 and 4 are connected to the line that leads to the terminal block at the next sensor location where these wires are connected to terminals 1 and 2 of *TB 2*. Again terminals 2 and 3 are strapped together and the branch line to the NC sensor is connected to terminals 3 and 4.

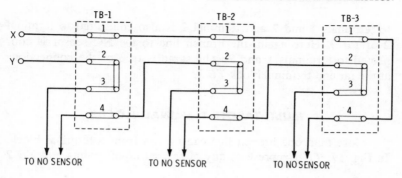

Fig. 15. Connections at closed-circuit sensor locations where four-terminal barrier blocks are used.

In this example, *TB 3* represents the terminal block at the far end of the line. Here, the main line is again connected to terminals 1 and 2 of *TB 3* and the branch line to the NC sensor to terminals 3 and 4. Terminals 2 and 3 are strapped as before. However, a wire jumper is used to strap terminals 1 and 4 to complete the closed circuit.

In lieu of using terminal blocks with four sets of terminals, blocks having only two sets of terminals can be used for tapping off branch lines to NC sensors as illustrated in Fig. 16. Here, one

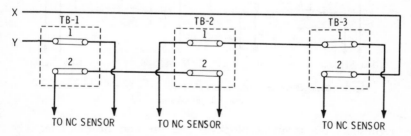

Fig. 16. Connections at closed-circuit sensor locations where two-terminal barrier blocks are used.

leg of the main line is run directly to terminal 2 of the far end terminal block *TB 3*. The other leg of the line is connected to terminal 1 of *TB 1*. The branch line to the NC sensor is connected

249

to terminals 1 and 2 and terminal 2 is also connected to terminal 2 of *TB 2*. Here again, the branch line to the NC sensor is connected to terminals 1 and 2. The same is true of the connections at the far end terminal block *TB 3*.

MULTI-TAPOFF TERMINAL BLOCKS

More than one branch line can be run from a terminal block. In Fig. 17, *TB 1* represents any of several tapoff points and *TB 2*

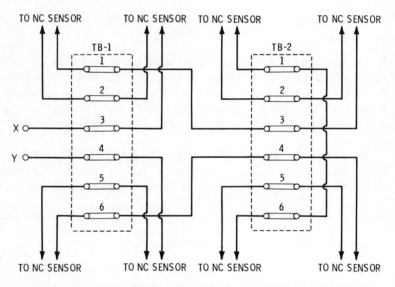

Fig. 17. Connections at barrier-terminal blocks when branch lines are run to closed-circuit sensors.

represents the terminal block at the far end of the line. The connections at *TB 2* differ from those at *TB 1* in that terminal 1 is jumped through a wire to terminal 6 since this diagram is of a closed-circuit system employing NC sensors.

Similar techniques can be used in an open-circuit system employing NO sensors. As shown in Fig. 18, three branch lines are run from *TB 1* and three branch lines are run from *TB 2*. At both terminal blocks, terminals 1, 3, 5 and 7 are jumped together by wires as are terminals 2, 4, 6 and 8.

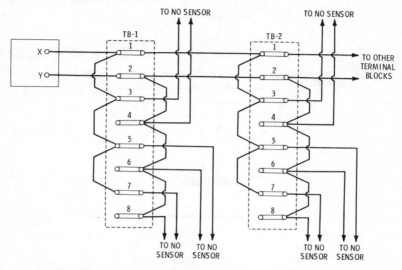

Fig. 18. Connections at barrier-terminal block when branch lines are run to open-circuit sensors.

The advantage of using terminal blocks should be obvious. Lines can be easily disconnected and re-connected when necessary. Also, a defective sensor can be disconnected readily. In the case of a defective NC sensor, the terminals to which the sensors branch line is connected can be jumpered. For example, in Fig. 17 if the sensor connected to terminals 5 and 6 of *TB 1* is defective, the leads to the sensor can be disconnected and a jumper can be connected across terminals 5 and 6 to keep the rest of the system intact.

CONDUIT WIRING

When terminal blocks are not used and the wires are run through conduit, leads can be connected together within conduit boxes by twisting their uninsulated ends and covering each splice with a plastic screw-on insulators as shown in Fig. 19. The connections at a NO sensor junction (bridging) point are shown in Fig. 19A, and at the end of a line in Fig. 19B.

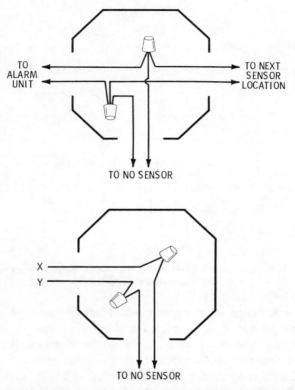

TO ALARM UNIT

TO NEXT SENSOR LOCATION

TO NO SENSOR

X

Y

TO NO SENSOR

Fig. 19. Connections at conduit boxes when closed-circuit sensors are used.

Since NC sensors are usually connected in series in a closed-circuit system, the connections at each conduit box are made in a different manner. In Fig. 20A, one of the line conductors is run straight through (through a splice) and the other is split so connections can be made to a single NC sensor. When two NC sensors are to be connected to a closed-circuit line, the wires are connected as shown in Fig. 20B. At the far end of the line, a single NC sensor is connected as shown in Fig. 20C.

252

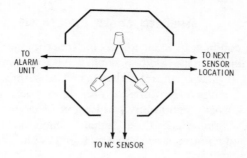

TO ALARM UNIT

TO NEXT SENSOR LOCATION

TO NC SENSOR

(A) Single-sensor tapoff.

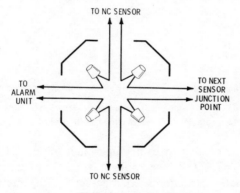

TO NC SENSOR

TO ALARM UNIT

TO NEXT SENSOR JUNCTION POINT

TO NC SENSOR

(B) Dual-sensor tapoff.

(C) End-of-line point.

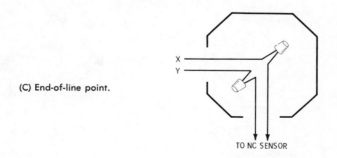

X

Y

TO NC SENSOR

Fig. 20. Connections at conduit boxes when open-circuit sensors are used.

253

SHIELDED CABLE JUNCTIONS

Single-conductor shielded cable (microphone, intercom or coaxial cable) can be used to connect NO or variable-resistance sensors to an alarm control unit when it is permissible to use an unbalanced transmission line. At a bridging point, a junction box is required. This junction box can be any metal box or a Pomona "black box" on which three female single-pin connectors are mounted and connected as shown in Fig. 21. The center conductor

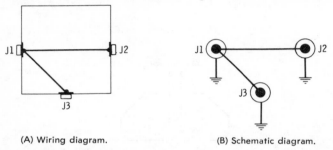

(A) Wiring diagram.   (B) Schematic diagram.

Fig. 21. Connections at single-tap junction box for open-circuit sensors when single-conductor shielded cable is used.

of the cables is connected to a plug which mates with the female connectors (*J1, J2, J3*). The cable shield is the return conductor. The cable shields are connected together by the metal box. The

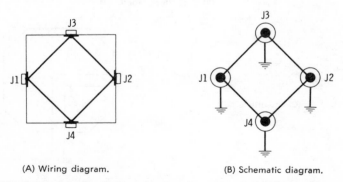

(A) Wiring diagram.   (B) Schematic diagram.

Fig. 22. Connections at dual-tap junction box for open-circuit sensors when single-conductor shielded cable is used.

254

female connectors and male plugs may be type F, N, UHF, micro-phone or other type designed for use with single-conductor shielded cable or coaxial cable.

Where two sensors are to be bridged across a line at the same point, the junction box should have four female connectors, as shown in Fig. 22.

Two-conductor shielded cable (microphone, intercom or video-pair cable) can be used for connecting NC sensors to an alarm control unit in a closed-circuit system. Fig. 23 shows the con-

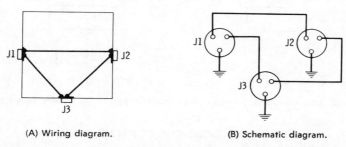

(A) Wiring diagram.

(B) Schematic diagram.

Fig. 23. Connections at single-tap junction box for closed-circuit sensors when two-conductor shielded or unshielded cable is used.

nections within a junction box for use at a single NC sensor tap-off point. Three 3-terminal female connectors are required. Two

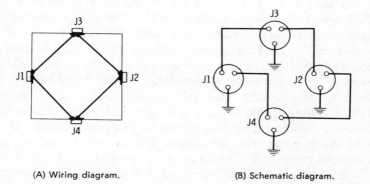

(A) Wiring diagram.

(B) Schematic diagram.

Fig. 24. Connections at dual-tap junction boxes for closed-circuit sensors.

of the terminals are used for conveying the signal and the third is used for extending the continuity of the cable shields.

The connections within a dual NC sensor tapoff junction box are shown in Fig. 24. In this example, one sensor is inserted in series with one leg of the line and the second sensor in the other leg.

The cables are connected to the junction boxes (in either Fig. 23 or Fig. 24) through matching three-pin plugs which are connected as shown in Fig. 25.

(A) Unshielded two-wire cable.   (B) Shielded two-conductor cable

Fig. 25 Cable connections to plugs when circuits shown in Fig. 23 and 24 are used.

ALARM LOCATION CONNECTIONS

In many instances, the line to a bell or other alarm device can be connected directly to it. However, from the standpoint of maintenance and troubleshooting it is more convenient to use terminal blocks. For example, a line running to a bell can be run to a terminal block with two sets of terminals with the line connected to terminals 1 and 2 and the bell also connected to terminals 1 and 2. When the line to the alarm is so long that voltage drop is excessive, an interposing relay and a local battery can be utilized as shown in Fig. 26. Here the line from the alarm unit is connected to terminals 1 and 2 of the terminal block. The winding of the relay K is also connected to terminals 1 and 2. A dry battery, the local power source, is connected to terminals 3 and 4 and the bell or horn to terminals 4 and 5 as shown. When there is voltage across terminals 1 and 2, as would be the case when the alarm unit has been triggered, the relay is pulled in and its NC contacts close and complete the circuit to the alarm device. As soon as the alarm condition has been corrected, the relay will drop out and its contacts will reopen. Switch S is a momentary contact NO

256

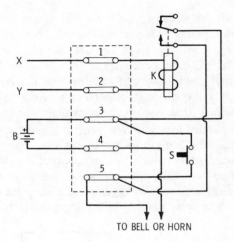

Fig. 26. Connections at terminal block at a bell or horn location when a local battery is used.

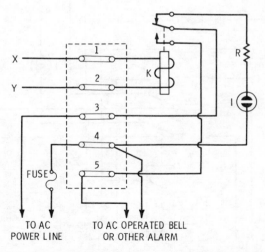

Fig. 27. Connections at terminal block at an AC-operated alarm location.

push button which can be used for testing the battery and alarm device.

When an AC operated bell or other alarm device is used, the wiring shown in Fig. 27 can be utilized. Here again, the relay is energized by a voltage from the alarm unit. When the relay is energized, its NO contacts complete the circuit to the alarm device. Under normal conditions, when the relay is not energized, its back contacts apply AC through a current limiting resistor to a neon lamp to indicate that AC power is available at this location.

Another alarm location arrangement is illustrated in Fig. 28. In this example, the bell or other alarm device is energized by a local storage battery which is kept charged by a trickle charger. Under normal conditions, relay K is de-energized and its back contacts energize a low-wattage incandescent pilot lamp to indicate that DC power is available. The resistance R in series with the

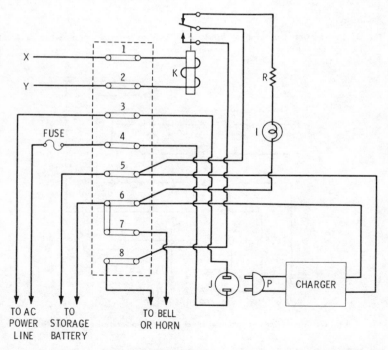

Fig. 28. Connections at terminal block at an alarm location where a storage battery and charger are used.

lamp, reduces lamp current and therefore extends its life. The input to the battery charger is connected through its power plug *P* to AC receptacle *J* which is connected to the AC line through terminals 3 and 4 of the terminal block. When an alarm condition exists, the relay is pulled in and its NO contacts close to complete the path to the alarm device. Using this arrangement, the alarm device will be energized whether AC power is available or not. The charger is one of the trickle charge or automatic type which can be left connected to the battery at all times.

INTERFERENCE SUPPRESSION

Long unshielded lines can pick up electrical noise and radio signals. In most cases, this is of no significance. However, in the case of sensitive sensors, noise and radio signal pickup can cause problems. Sometimes these problems are introduced by switch type sensors. If the sensor contacts do not have low resistance when closed, often due to dirt or accumulation of film, they can act as rectifiers and demodulate radio signals, resulting in the application of the DC voltage across the line. The effects of unwanted pickup of noise and radio signals can be alleviated or totally eliminated by installing filters. When NC sensors are used, the filter

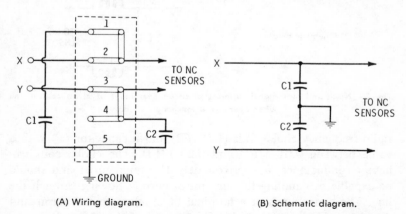

(A) Wiring diagram.   (B) Schematic diagram.

Fig. 29. Noise and radio-signal suppression circuit near input of alarm control unit when closed-circuit sensors are used.

259

can consist of a pair of capacitors (0.01 - 0.25 MFD) connected at a terminal block as shown in Fig. 29A and as shown schematically in Fig. 29B. The series connected capacitors are connected across the main line with their junction point connected to an earth ground. The terminal block may be located close to the alarm unit with the line running to the terminal blocks at sensor locations connected to terminals 2 and 3 of the terminal block.

When NO sensors are used, the filter arrangement shown in Fig. 30 can be used. In this example, the filter consists of two

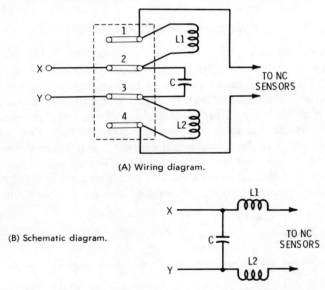

(A) Wiring diagram.

(B) Schematic diagram.

Fig. 30. Noise and radio-signal suppression circuit near input of alarm control unit when open-circuit sensors are used.

radio frequency choke coils ($L1$ - $L2$) and a capacitor (C) with a value between 0.01 MFD and 0.25 MFD. The choke coils can have an inductance of approximately 100 millihenries and should be capable of handling the amount of current flowing through the line. The connections at a terminal block close to the alarm unit are shown in Fig. 30A and the schematic of the circuit is shown in Fig. 30B.

COAXIAL CABLE TAPS

When coaxial cable is used for transmission of alarm and/or television signals, connections to the cable are made through appropriate quick-disconnect connectors. In lieu of using a terminal block at a connection point, a wall plate equipped with a female coaxial connector, such as the one shown in Fig. 31, can be used.

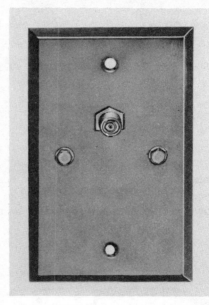

Fig. 31. Coaxial cable tapoff.

The center conductor of the coaxial cable is soldered to the center terminal of the coaxial outlet and the shield of the coaxial cable is soldered to the shell of the coaxial cable outlet. The connections are made at the back of the plate and are not shown in the illustration.

At a tapoff point where the coaxial line is to be continued on to other points, a coaxial cable tapoff device such as the one shown in Fig. 32 can be used. This device has three female coaxial connectors to which the coaxial plugs are connected. The incoming line is connected to the jack at the left and the outgoing cable to the jack at the right. The tapoff cable is connected to the center jack.

261

FLEXIBLE CONNECTORS

Sensors or other devices attached to a door or other place where movement of one part of the circuit is required should be

Fig. 32. Coaxial cable inline tap.

connected through a flexible cable designed for that specific purpose. Fig. 33 shows two examples of door cords. The one shown in Fig. 33A is designed to be permanently connected. The

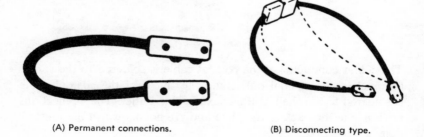

(A) Permanent connections.

(B) Disconnecting type.

Courtesy Electronic Instrument Co.

Fig. 33. Door cords.

one shown in Fig. 33B consists of two sections with quick-disconnect connectors. The two sections can be disconnected and reconnected at will.

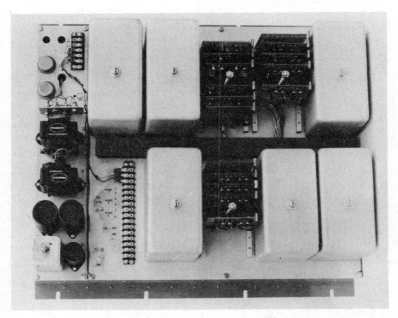

Fig. 34. Alarm control unit showing barrier-terminal blocks for external connections and plug-in printed-circuit boards.

ALARM UNIT CONNECTIONS

An example of alarm control unit construction is shown in Fig. 34. The electronic circuit components are mounted on plug-in printed circuit cords which can be easily removed or replaced if necessary. As can be seen in the illustration, screw terminals are provided for external connections.

Fig. 35 shows the drawing on the rear of the front panel of an alarm control unit. The drawing shows the locations of the screw terminals and their identification. This type of construction makes it easier to achieve a professional caliber installation.

DOORBELL INTERCOM CIRCUIT

To determine who is at the door of a residence, a conventional wired intercom or CCTV system can be installed. Or, the telephone

263

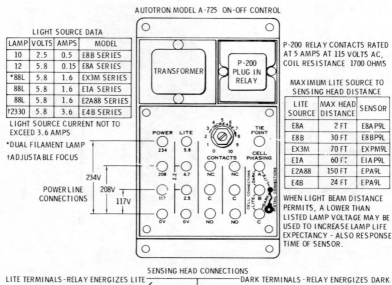

AUTOTRON MODEL A-725 ON-OFF CONTROL

LIGHT SOURCE DATA

LAMP	VOLTS	AMPS	MODEL
10	2.5	0.5	E8B SERIES
12	5.8	0.15	E8A SERIES
*88L	5.8	1.6	EX3M SERIES
88L	5.8	1.6	E1A SERIES
88L	5.8	1.6	E2A88 SERIES
†2330	5.8	3.6	E4B SERIES

LIGHT SOURCE CURRENT NOT TO
EXCEED 3.6 AMPS

*DUAL FILAMENT LAMP

†ADJUSTABLE FOCUS

POWER LINE CONNECTIONS

234V
208V
117V

TRANSFORMER

P-200 PLUG IN RELAY

P-200 RELAY CONTACTS RATED
AT 5 AMPS AT 115 VOLTS AC,
COIL RESISTANCE 1700 OHMS

MAXIMUM LITE SOURCE TO
SENSING HEAD DISTANCE

LITE SOURCE	MAX HEAD DISTANCE	SENSOR
E8A	2 FT	E8AP9L
E8B	30 FT	E8BP9L
EX3M	70 FT	EXPM9L
E1A	60 FT	E1AP9L
E2A88	150 FT	EPA9L
E4B	24 FT	EPA9L

WHEN LIGHT BEAM DISTANCE
PERMITS, A LOWER THAN
LISTED LAMP VOLTAGE MAY BE
USED TO INCREASE LAMP LIFE
EXPECTANCY - ALSO RESPONSE
TIME OF SENSOR.

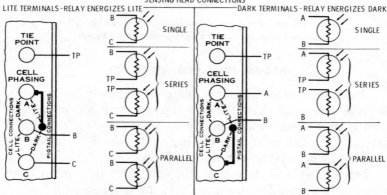

SENSING HEAD CONNECTIONS

LITE TERMINALS - RELAY ENERGIZES LITE

DARK TERMINALS - RELAY ENERGIZES DARK

SINGLE

SERIES

PARALLEL

SERIES SENSOR CONNECTION REDUCES MAX HEAD DISTANCE APPROXIMATELY 35%
NO POLARITY FOR HEADS
MAX HEAD DISTANCE REDUCES APPROXIMATELY 50% WITH INFRARED LIGHT

Courtesy Autotron, Inc.

Fig. 35. Drawing of front panel of an alarm control unit showing screw terminals for external connections.

company can furnish and install an intercom system. When it is inconvenient (or too expensive) to run wires to an intercom slave

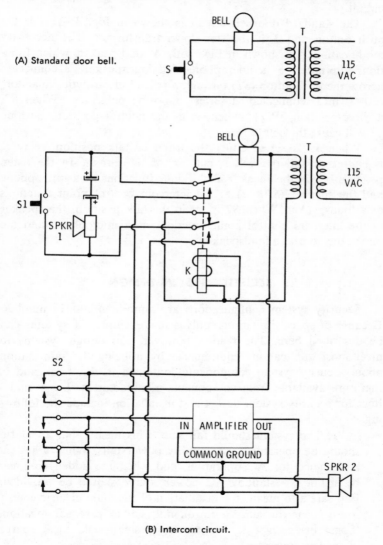

(A) Standard door bell.

(B) Intercom circuit.

Fig. 36. Combination door bell and intercom circuit.

unit at an entrance door where there is already a doorbell push button, an intercom system can be superimposed on the doorbell circuit.

The standard doorbell circuit is shown in Fig. 36A; S is the push button and T is the step-down transformer. The necessary modifications are shown in Fig. 36B. A loudspeaker, which functions alternately as a microphone and loudspeaker, is connected across the pushbutton ($S1$) through a pair of electrolytic capacitors (20-40 mfd) connected in series (opposing polarities). When $S2$, a three-position 3PDT switch, is in the neutral position, pushing $S1$ will cause the bell to ring.

When $S2$ is set to either the listen or talk position, relay K is energized and the bell is cut out of the circuit. In the listen position of $S2$, the speaker at the door functions as a microphone and the speaker (SPK 2) at the intercom control point functions as a loudspeaker. When $S2$ is set in the talk position, the speaker at the intercom control point functions as a microphone and the one at the door as a loudspeaker.

SECURITY SYSTEM DESIGN

Security system configurations are almost endless in number. Because of space limitations, only a few examples of systems can be described here. The reader, however, can design systems to meet most application requirements by utilizing the information about security system components contained in this book and in literature available from components manufacturers. Basic guidelines for security system design and installation include the following.

1. The system should fail safe. This means that an alarm should be operable even if utility power fails. When a system is designed for AC operation, and when the added cost can be justified, a standby AC power source should be provided. Fail-safe also means the installation of the main electric energy source near the alarm control unit, not at a sensor location. (Some bridge-type sensor require a small-scale local source of electric power.)

2. The alarm devices should be installed where they are not easily accessible to intruders, and the wires run to them should preferably be concealed.

3. Sensors should be installed in such a manner that their presence is not immediately obvious, or so that they can't be tampered without attracting attention.

4. Wiring should also be installed so its presence is not obvious or so that it is not easily accessible to intruders. When economically feasible, armored cable or conduit should be used, except for short runs to door and window sensors.

5. Maintainability should be given careful consideration. Maintenance can be made easier by utilizing connecting devices in lieu of wire splices from which tape must be removed to gain access to the conductors.

The two examples of security systems discussed below differ in complexity. One is a home-type system that is purely electrical whereas the industrial-type system employs both electrical and electronic devices.

TYPICAL HOME SECURITY SYSTEM

The components of a typical home security system were previously identified in Fig. 1 of Chapter 1. The actual connections of a professionally-installed system are shown in Fig. 37. *TB-1* and *TB-2* are each in a bedroom, *TB-3* is a junction box, and *TB-4* and *TB-5* are in other rooms of a home or apartment.

Each of the bedrooms is equipped with a fire sensor (NO) and an NO panic button (*S1, S2*) plus an alarm horn. One of the other two rooms is equipped with an NC door sensor (*S4*) and a horn; the other room is equipped with two NC window sensors (*S5, S6*) and a relay (*K3*) for activating an automatic telephone dialing device.

When either of the fire sensors or *S1* or *S2* is closed, relay *K1* pulls in and energizes the horns and the telephone dialer actuating relay (*K3*). Or, when NC sensor *S4, S5,* or *S6* is opened, relay *K2* drops out and the horns and telephone dial actuating relay are energized.

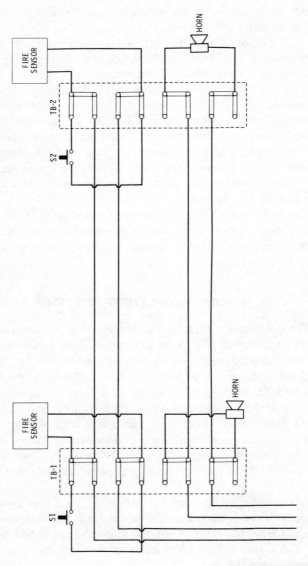

Fig. 37. Wiring diagram of a

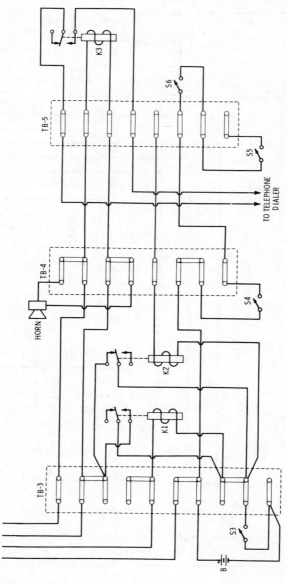

residential security system.

269

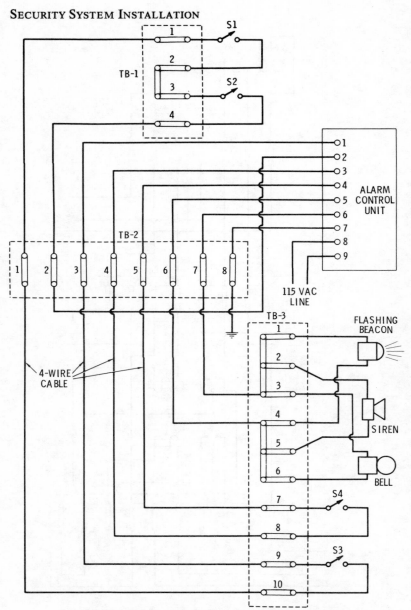

Fig. 38. Wiring diagram of a closed-circuit intrusion alarm system.

The system is energized by battery *B* (hotshot or lantern battery). Switch *S1* enables turning the system on or off. As can be noted in Fig. 36, only four-wire cables are required for interconnecting the terminal blocks.

TIME DELAY ALARM SYSTEM

A wiring diagram of an intrusion alarm, suitable for a store or other building with only two entrances, is shown in Fig. 38. It is based on the alarm system used at television station WKZT-TV as described in the magazine, Broadcast Engineering.

Switches *S1* and *S2* represent NC magnetic reed switches at the door and screen/storm door at the rear entrance. They are connected to barrier terminal block *TB-1* which in turn is connected through a two-wire cable to *TB-2* near the alarm control unit.

Switch *S3* is an NC switch at the front door and *S4* is an NO key lock switch near the front door. They are connected to *TB-3* and their circuits are extended to *TB-2* through a four-wire cable or a pair of two-wire cables.

Located near the front door, but inaccessible to prowlers on foot are a bell, siren and flashing beacon lamp, all connected to *TB-3* as shown. Their leads are strapped at *TB-3* as shown. From terminals 3 and 4 of *TB-3,* a pair of No. 14 or larger wires are run to *TB-2* (these wires should be run in accordance with local electrical codes). Terminal blocks *TB-2* and *TB-3* should be installed inside of metal boxes so their 115VAC terminals are not exposed. To make it more difficult for an intruder to bypass *S1* and *S2, TB-1* should also be inside of a metal box or otherwise concealed.

Terminals 2, 3, 4 and 5 of *TB-2* can be connected to the alarm control unit through a four-wire cable or a pair of two-wire cables to the terminals of the alarm control unit, as shown in the diagram. Terminals 6 and 7 of *TB-2* should be No. 14 or larger wire and, again, installed in accordance with local electrical codes. Terminal 8 is connected to an earth ground (optional) to ground the case of the alarm control unit.

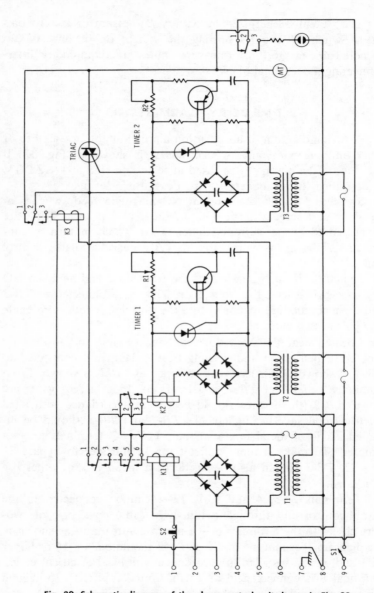

Fig. 39. Schematic diagram of the alarm control unit shown in Fig. 38.

The circuitry of the alarm control unit is shown in Fig. 39. Its terminals 8 and 9 are connected to the AC power line, directly or through an electric power outlet. It contains two electronic timing circuits, three relays, a motor-driven timing switch and three DC power supplies.

Normally, when the building is occupied, switch $S1$ is in the OFF (open) position so the system cannot operate. To arm the system, $S1$ is placed in the ON position and all personnel leave the building.

Closing $S1$ causes 115 VAC to be applied directly to the primary of transformer $T2$ and through the NC contacts (1-2) of relay $K2$ to the primary of $T1$. The 6-volt DC output of the bridge rectifier fed by $T2$ causes relay $K1$ to pull in (if all of the external NC sensors are closed). Contacts 5-6 of $K1$ close and latch this relay in the energized position. At the same time, 6 volts AC is fed from the secondary of $T2$ to the winding of relay $K3$ causing it to pull in and open its NC contacts (1-2).

After a delay of from 30 seconds to 3 minutes, depending upon the setting of timing control $R1$, relay $K2$ is energized. Its NC contacts (1-2) open and its NO contacts (2-3) close and apply 115 VAC to contact 2 of $K1$.

Now, the key switch ($S4$ in Fig. 38) is opened after the front door has been closed. This causes relay $K3$ (Fig. 39) to drop out and reclose its NC (1-2) contacts, short-circuiting the triac. The system is now "armed". Since relay $K1$ is energized and its 1-2 contacts are open, AC does not reach the triac, motor-driven timer (MT) nor the primary of $T3$.

If the NC test push button $S2$ or any of the sensors ($S1$, $S2$ or $S3$ in Fig. 38) is opened momentarily, or if the closed circuit loop wire is cut, the system will be triggered. Relay $K1$ (Fig. 39) drops out. Its 5-6 contacts open and cut off AC to the primary of $T1$. Its 1-2 contacts close and apply AC to the motor-driven timer motor and its contact No. 2, and to the primary of $T3$.

Contacts 1-2 of timer MT close and apply AC to the external bell, siren and flashing beacon. These alarms continue to operate until the motor-driven timer stops running (after about 10 minutes) and its 1-2 contacts open. Then, its 2-3 contacts close and apply

273

AC to neon lamp *I* which will continue to glow and indicates that the system had been triggered.

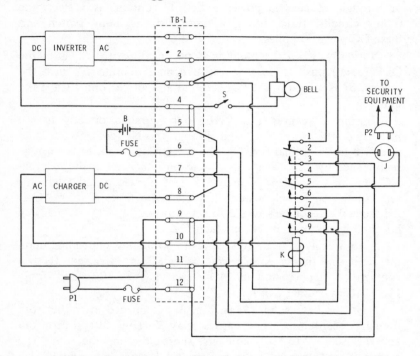

Fig. 40. Standby power supply system for an AC operated security system.

To enter the building without tripping the alarm immediately, the key switch (*S4* in Fig. 38) is closed. This causes relay *K3* (Fig. 39) to pull in and open its NC contacts (1-2) and remove the short from across the triac. Since opening the door causes *S3* (Fig. 38) to open and thus cause relay *K1* (Fig. 39) to drop out and close its NC contacts (1-2), the alarms would be turned on if it were not for electronic timer 2. The person entering the building must hurry to turn off *S1* (Fig. 39) before timer 2 triggers the triac. If *S1* is not turned off before the triac is triggered, power will be applied (through the triac) to the motor-driven timer and the alarms.

STANDBY ELECTRIC POWER

Although a security system can be designed to operate only from power furnished by dry batteries, the system capabilities and scope are limited by the current capacity of the batteries. Furthermore, dry batteries deteriorate whether used or not. Lead-acid storage batteries can be used instead, but they require recharging. This can be accomplished by connecting the DC output of a trickle charger across the battery terminals.

An AC-operated security system (even a CCTV system) can be operated from power furnished by a storage battery during times when utility power fails. Fig. 40 shows the wiring of a standby electric power system.

Normally, AC from the power line is obtained from an electric outlet through plug $P1$ (or through a direct connection to the power line) and fed through NO contacts 2-3 and 5-6 of relay K to AC receptacle J to which the security equipment is connected via plug $P2$.

Since the winding of AC-operated relay K is normally energized by AC from the power line, its contacts 2-3, 5-6 and 8-9 are held closed. Contacts 8-9 connect the + terminal of the 12-volt storage battery (B) to the output of the battery charger whose input is connected to the AC power line through terminal block TB.

In the event of AC power line failure, the relay drops out. Contacts 7-8 close to apply DC from the battery to the input of the DC-to-AC inverter. Contacts 1-2 and 4-5 close to apply the AC output of the inverter to the security equipment. Contacts 7-8 also apply DC to the alarm bell which can be turned off with switch S. As soon as utility power is restored, the relay is again energized. The inverter is automatically turned off and the AC input to the security system is transferred from the output of the inverter back to the AC power line.

Index

AUDEL BOOKS *practical reading for profit*

APPLIANCES

Air Conditioning (23159)

Domestic, commercial, and automobile air conditioning fully explained in easily-understood language. Troubleshooting charts aid in making diagnosis and repair of system troubles.

Home Appliance Servicing (23016)

A practical "How-To-Do-It" book for electric & gas servicemen, mechanics & dealers. Covers principles, servicing and repairing of home appliances. Tells how to locate troubles, make repairs, reassemble and connect, wiring diagrams and testing methods. Tells how to fix electric refrigerators, washers, ranges, toasters, ironers, broilers, dryers, vacuums, fans, and other appliances.

Home Refrigeration and Air Conditioning (23133)

Covers basic principles, servicing, operation, and repair of modern household refrigerators and air conditioners. Automotive air conditioners are also included. Troubleshooting charts aid in trouble diagnosis. **A gold mine of essential facts for engineers, servicemen, and users.**

Oil Burners (23151)

Provides complete information on all types of oil burners and associated equipment. Discusses burners—blowers—ignition transformers—electrodes—nozzles—fuel pumps—filters controls. Installation and maintenance are stressed. Troubleshooting charts permit rapid diagnosis of system troubles and possible remedies to correct them.

AUTOMOTIVE

Automobile Guide (23192)

New revised edition. Practical reference for auto mechanics, servicemen, trainees, and owners. Explains theory, construction, and servicing of modern domestic motorcars. FEATURES: All parts of an automobile—engines—pistons—rings—connecting rods—crankshafts—valves—cams—timing—cooling systems—Fuel-feed systems—carbureators — automatic choke — transmissions — clutches — universals — propeller shafts—dierentials—rear axles—running gear—brakes—wheel alignment—steering gear—tires—lubrication—ignition systems—generators and alternators—starters—lighting systems—batteries—air conditioning—cruise controls—emission control systems.

Auto Engine Tune-up (23181)

New revised edition. This popular how-to-do-it guide shows exactly how to tune your car engine for extra power, gas economy, and fewer costly repairs. New emission-control systems are explained along with the proper methods for correcting faults and making adjustments to keep these systems in top operating condition.

Automotive Library—2 Vols. (23198)

Diesel Engine Manual (23199)

A practical treatise on the theory, operation and maintenance of modern Diesel engines. Explains Diesel principles—valves—timing—fuel pumps—pistons and rings—cylinders—lubrication—cooling system—fuel oil—engine indicator—governors—engine reversing—answers on operation—calculations. AN IMPORTANT GUIDE FOR ENGINEERS, OPERATORS, STUDENTS.

Foreign Auto Repair Manual (23078)

Contains complete, service and repair data for the most popular imported makes, including Fiat, Hillman Minx, M.G., Opel, Peugot, Renault, SAAB, Simca, Volkswagen, and Volvo. Introductory chapters provide complete data on operation and maintenance of fuel and ignition systems.

Gas Engine Manual (23061)

A completely practical book covering the construction, operation and repair of all types of modern gas engines. Part I covers gas-engine principles; engine parts; auxiliaries; timing methods; ignition systems. Part II covers troubleshootng, adjustment and repairs.

Truck & Tractor Guide (23020)

A shop companion for truck mechanics and drivers—shop foremen—garagemen—maintenance men—helpers—owners—troubleshooters—fleet maintenance men—bus mechanics and drivers—farm tractor operators and mechanics. Covers gas and diesel motor principles—construction—operation—miantenance—repair—service operations—troubleshooting—engine tune-up—carburetor adjusting—ignition tuning—brakes—service of all parts.—1001 FACTS AT YOUR FINGER TIPS.

BUILDING AND MAINTENANCE

Answers on Blueprint Reading (23041)

Covers all types of blueprint reading for mechanics and builders. The man who can read blueprints is in line for a better job. This book gives you the secret language, step by step in easy stages. NO OTHER TRADE BOOK LIKE IT.

Builders Encyclopedia (23178)

A book of terms used by members of the building and construction trade. A valuable book for the carpenter, plumber, electrician, steel erector, bridge builder, general contractor, architect and others in the building and construction industry.

Building Construction and Design (23180)

A completely revised and rewritten version of Audel's **Architects and Builders Guide.** New illustrations and extended coverage of material makes this treatment of the subject more valuable than ever. Anyone connected in any way with the building industry will profit from the information contained in this book.

Building Maintenance (23140)

A comprehensive book on the practical aspects of building maintenance. Chapters are included on: painting and decorating; plumbing and pipe fitting; carpentry; calking and glazing; concrete and masonry; roofing; sheet metal; electrical maintenance; air conditioning and refrigeration; insect and rodent control; heating maintenance management; cutodial practices: A BOOK FOR BUILDING OWNERS, MANAGERS, AND MAINTENANCE PERSONNEL.

Grounds Maintenance (23186)

A comprehensive guide for the homeowner, industrial, municipal, and estate groundskeepers. Information on proper care of annual and perennial flowers; various house plants; greenhouse design and construction; insect and rodent control; complete lawn care; shrubs and trees; and maintenance of walks, roads, and traffic areas. Various types of maintenance equipment are also discussed.

Building- and Grounds-Maintenance Library— 2 Vols. (23197)

Carpenters & Builders Library—4 Vols. (23169)

A practical illustrated trade assistant on modern construction for carpenters, builders, and all woodworkers. Explains in practical, concise language and illustrations all the principles, advances and short cuts based on modern practice. How to calculate various jobs.
Vol. 1—(23170)—Tools, steel square, saw filing, joinery, cabinets.
Vol. 2—(23171)—Mathematics, plans, specifications, estimates.
Vol. 3—(23172)—House and roof framing, laying out, foundations.
Vol. 4—(23173)—Doors, windows, stairs, millwork, painting.

Carpentry and Building (23142)

Answers to the problems encountered in today's building trades. The actual questions asked of an architect by carpenters and builders are answered in this book. No apprentice or journeyman carpenter should be without the help this book can offer.

Commercial Refrigeration (23195)

Installation, operation, and repair of commercial refrigeration systems. Included are ice-making plants, locker plants, grocery and supermarket refrigerated display cases, etc. Trouble charts aid in the diagnosis and repair of defective systems.

Do-It-Yourself Encyclopedia (23207)

An all-in-one home repair and project guide for all do-it-yourselfers. Packed with step-by-step plans, thousands of photos, helpful charts. A really authentic, truly monumental, home-repair and home-project guide.

Home Workshop & Tool Handy Book (23208)

The most modern, up-to-date manual ever designed for home craftsmen and do-it-yourselfers. Tells how to set up your own home workshop, (basement, garage, or spare room), all about the various hand and power tools (when, where, and how to use them, etc.). Covers both wood- and metal-working principles and practices. An all-in-one workshop guide for handy men, professionals and students.

Plumbers and Pipe Fitters Library—3 Vols. (23155)

A practical illustrated trade assistant and reference for master plumbers, journeyman and apprentice pipe fitters, gas fitters and helpers, builders, contractors, and engineers. Explains in simple language, illustrations, diagrams, charts, graphs and pictures, the principles of modern plumbing and pipe-fitting practices.
Vol. 1—(23152)—Materials, tools, calculations.
Vol. 2—(23153)—Drainage, fittings, fixtures.
Vol. 3—(23154)—Installation, heating, welding.

Masons and Builders Library—2 Vols. (23185)

A practical illustrated trade assistant on modern construction for bricklayers, stonemasons, cement workers, plasterers, and tile setters. Explains in clear language and with detailed illustrations all the principles, advances, and shortcuts based on modern practice—including how to figure and calculate various jobs.
Vol. 1—(23182)—Concrete, Block, Tile, Terrazzo.
Vol. 2—(23183)—Bricklaying, Plastering, Rock Masonry, Clay Tile.

Upholstering (23189)

Upholstering is explained for the average householder and apprentice upholsterer in this Audel text. Selection of coverings, stuffings, springs, and other upholstering material is made simple. From repairing and reglueing of the bare frame, to the final sewing or tacking, for antiques and most modern pieces, this book gives complete and clearly written instructions and numerous illustrations.

ELECTRICITY-ELECTRONICS

Wiring Diagrams for Light & Power   (23028)

Electricians, wiremen, linemen, plant superintendents, construction engineers, electrical contractors, and students will find these diagrams a valuable source of practical help. Each diagram is complete and self-explaining. A PRACTICAL HANDY BOOK OF ELECTRICAL HOOK-UPS.

Electric Motors   (23150)

Covers the construction, theory of operation, connection, control, maintenance, and troubleshooting of all types of electric motors. A HANDY GUIDE FOR ELECTRICIANS AND ALL ELECTRICAL WORKERS.

Practical Electricity   (23160)

This updated version is a ready reference book, giving complete instruction and practical information on the rules and laws of electricity—maintenance of electrical machinery—AC and DC motors—wiring diagrams—lighting—house and power wiring —meter and instrument connections—transformer connectors—circuit breakers— power stations—automatic substations. THE KEY TO A PRACTICAL UNDERSTANDING OF ELECTRICITY.

House Wiring—2nd Edition   (23190)

Answers many questions in plain simple language concerning all phases of house wiring. A ready reference book with over 100 illustrations and concise interpretations of many rulings contained in the National Electrical Code. Electrical contractors, wiremen, and electricians will find this book invaluable as a tool in the electrical field

Guide to the 1971 National Electric Code   (23193)

This important and informative book is now revised to conform to the 1971 National Electrical Code. Offers an interpretation and simplification of the rulings contained in the Code. Electrical contractors, wiremen, and electricians will find this book invaluable for a more complete understanding of the NEC.

Questions and Answers for Electrical Examinations   (23200)

Newly revised to conform to the 1971 National Electrical Code. A practical book to help you prepare for all grades of electricians examinations. A helpful review of fundamental principles underlying each question and answer needed to prepare you to solve any new or similar problem. Covers the NEC; questions and answers for license tests; Ohm's law with applied examples, hook-ups for motors, lighting, and instruments. A COMPLETE REVIEW FOR ALL ELECTRICAL WORKERS.

Electrical Library—6 Vols.   (23194)

Electric Generating Systems   (23179)

Answers many questions concerning the selection, installation, operation, and maintenance of engine-driven electric generating systems for emergency, standby, and away-from-the-power-line applications. Private homes, hospitals, radio and television stations, and pleasure boats are only a few of the installations that owners either desire or require for primary power or for standby use in case of commercial power failure. THE MOST COMPREHENSIVE COVERAGE OF THIS SUBJECT TO BE FOUND TODAY.

Electrical Power Calculations   (23050)

275 TYPICAL PROBLEMS WORKED OUT. Presents and explains the mathematical formulas and the fundamental electrical laws for all the everday, practical problems in both AC and DC electricity. EVERY ELECTRICAL WORKER AND STUDENT NEEDS THIS MODERN MATHEMATICAL TOOL.

New Electric Library

For engineers, electricians, electrical workers, mechanics and students. Presenting in simple, concise form the fundamental principles, rules and applications of applied electricity. Fully illustrated with diagrams and sketches, also calculations and tables for ready reference. Based on the best knowledge and experience of applied electricity.

ENGINEERS-MECHANICS-MACHINISTS
Machinists Library   (23174)

Covers modern machine-shop practice. Tells how to set up and operate lathes, screw and milling machines, shapers, drill presses and all other machine tools. A complete reference library. A SHOP COMPANION THAT ANSWERS YOUR QUESTIONS.

Vol. 1—(23175)--Basic Machine Shop.
Vol. 2--(23176)--Machine Shop.
Vol. 3—(23177)--Toolmakers Handy Book

Millwrights and Mechanics Guide—
2nd Edition   (23201)

Practical information on plant installation, operation, and maintenance for Millwrights, mechanics, maintenance men, erectors, riggers, foremen, inspectors, and superintendents. Partial contents: • Drawing and Sketching • Machinery Installation • Power-Transmission Equipment • Couplings • Packing and Seals • Bearings • Structural Steel • Mechanical Fasteners • Pipe Fittings and Valves • Carpentry • Sheet-Metal Work • Blacksmithing • Rigging • Electricity • Welding • Mathematics and much more.

Practical Guide to Mechanics   (23102)

A Convenient reference book valuable for its practical and concise explanations of the applicable laws of physics. Presents all the basics of mechanics in everyday language, illustrated with practical examples of their applications in various fields.

Questions & Answers for Engineers
and Firemans Examinations   (23053)

An aid for stationary, marine, diesel & hoisting engineers' examinations for all grades of licenses. A new concise review explaining in detail the principles, facts and figures of practical engineering. Questions & Answers.

Welders Guide—2nd Edition (23202)

New revised edition. Covers principles of electric, oxyacetylene, thermit, unionmelt welding for sheet metal; spot and pipe welds; pressure vessels; aluminum, copper brass, bronze, plastics, and other metals; airplane work; surface hardening and hard facing; cutting brazing; underwater welding; eye protection. EVERY WELDER SHOULD OWN THIS GUIDE.

FLUID POWER
Practical Guide to Fluid Power   (23136)

An essential book for the owner, operator, supervisor, or maintenance man concerned with hydraulic or pneumatic equipment. A complete coverage of modern design, application, and repair of fluid power devices. Fully illustrated.

Pumps (23167)

A detailed book on all types of pumps from the old-fashioned kitchen variety to the most modern types. Covers construction, application, installation, and troubleshooting.

MATHEMATICS

Practical Mathematics for Everyone—2 Vols. (23112)

A concise and reliable guide to the understanding of practical mathematics. People from all walks of life, young and old alike, will find the information contained in these two books just what they have been looking for. The mathematics discussed is for the everyday problems that arise in every household and business.
Vol. 1—(23110)—Basic Mathematics.
Vol. 2—(23111)—Financial Mathematics.

OUTBOARD MOTORS

Outboard Motors & Boating (23168)

Provides the information necessary to adjust, repair, and maintain all types of outboard motors. Valuable information concerning boating rules and regulations is also included.

RADIO-TELEVISION-AUDIO

Handbook of Commercial Sound Installations (23126)

A practical complete guide to planning commercial systems, selecting the most suitable equipment, and following through with the most proficient servicing methods. For technicians and the professional and businessman interested in installing a sound system.

Practical Guide to Auto Radio Repair (23128)

A complete servicing guide for all types of auto radios, including hybrid, all-transistor, and FM . . . PLUS removal instructions for all late-model radios. Fully illustrated.

Practical Guide to Servicing Electronic Organs (23132)

Detailed, illustrated discussions of the operation and servicing of electronic organs. Including models by Allen, Baldwin, Conn, Hammond, Kinsman, Lowrey, Magnavox, Thomas, and Wurlitzer.

Radioman's Guide (23163)

Audel best-seller, containing the latest information on radio and electronics from the basics through transistors. Covers radio fundamentals—Ohm's law—physics of sound as related to radio—radio-wave transmission—test equipment—power supplies—resistors, inductors, and capacitors—transformers—vacuum tubes—transistors—speakers—antennas—troubleshooting. A complete guide and a perfect preliminary to the study of television servicing.

Television Service Manual (23162)

Includes the latest designs and information. Thoroughly covers television with transmitter theory, antenna designs, receiver circuit operation and the picture tube. Provides the practical information necessary for accurate diagnosis and repair of both black-and-white and color television receivers. A MUST BOOK FOR ANYONE IN TELEVISION.

Radio-TV Library—2 Vol. (23161)

SHEET METAL

Sheet Metal Workers Handy Book (23046)

Containing practical information and important facts and figures. Easy to understand. Fundamentals of sheet metal layout work. Clearly written in everyday language. Ready reference index.

TO ORDER AUDEL BOOKS mail this handy form to

Theo. Audel & Co., 4300 W. 62nd
Indianapolis, Indiana 46268

Please send me for FREE EXAMINATION books marked (x) below. If I decide to keep them I agree to mail $3 in 10 days on each book or set ordered and further mail ⅓ of the total purchase price 30 days later, with the balance plus shipping costs to be mailed within another 30 days. Otherwise, I will return them for refund.

APPLIANCES
- ☐ (23159) Air Conditioning .... $ 5.95
- ☐ (23016) Home Appliance Servicing 6.95
- ☐ (23133) Home Refrigeration and
  Air Conditioning 6.95
- ☐ (23151) Oil Burners 5.50

AUTOMOTIVE
- ☐ (23198) Automotive Library (2 Vols.) 12.50
  - ☐ (23192) Automobile Guide 8.95
  - ☐ (23181) Auto Engine Tune-Up 5.95
- ☐ (23024) Diesel Engine Manual 6.95
- ☐ (23078) Foreign Auto Repair Manual 5.95
- ☐ (23061) Gas Engine Manual 4.95
- ☐ (23020) Truck and Tractor Guide 7.50

BUILDING AND MAINTENANCE
- ☐ (23041) Answers on Blueprint Reading 5.25
- ☐ (23178) Builders Encyclopedia 7.95
- ☐ (23180) Building Construction and
  Design 5.95
- ☐ (23197) Building- and Grounds-Main-
  tenance Library (2 Vols.) .. 12.95
  - ☐ (23140) Building Maintenance 5.95
  - ☐ (23186) Grounds Maintenance 7.95
- ☐ (23169) Carpenters and Builders
  Library (4 Vols.) 18.50
  - ☐ Single Volumes sold separately .... ea. 4.95
  - ☐ (23142) Carpentry and Building 5.95
  - ☐ (23195) Commercial Refrigeration 6.50
- ☐ (23207) Do-it-Yourself Encyclopedia 10.50
- ☐ (23208) Home Workshop & Tool
  Handy Book 5.00
- ☐ (23185) Masons & Builders Library
  (2 Vols.) 11.25
  - ☐ Single Volumes sold separately .... ea. 5.95
- ☐ (23189) Upholstering 5.95
- ☐ (23155) Plumbers and Pipe Fitters
  Library (3 Vols.) 13.50
  - ☐ Single Volumes sold separately .... ea. 4.95

ELECTRICITY-ELECTRONICS
- ☐ (23179) Electric Generating Systems 5.95
- ☐ (23194) Electrical Library (6 Vols.) 29.95
  - ☐ (23028) Wiring Diagrams for
    Light and Power 5.50
  - ☐ (23150) Electric Motors 5.95
  - ☐ (23160) Practical Electricity 5.95

- ☐ (23190) House Wiring (2nd Edition) 5.95
- ☐ (23193) Guide to the 1971 National
  Electrical Code 6.95
- ☐ (23200) Questions & Answers for
  Electrician's Exams 4.50
- ☐ (23050) Electrical Power Calculations 4.50

NEW ELECTRIC LIBRARY
- ☐ Single Volumes sold separately ....ea. 4.00

ENGINEERS-MECHANICS-MACHINISTS
- ☐ (23174) Machinists Library (3 Vols.) 16.95
  - ☐ Single Volumes sold separately ...ea. 5.95
- ☐ (23202) Welders Guide (2nd Edition) 9.95
- ☐ (23201) Millwrights and Mechanics
  Guide (2nd Edition) 9.95
- ☐ (23102) Practical Guide to Mechanics 4.95
- ☐ (23053) Q&A for Engineers and
  Firemans Exams 5.50

FLUID POWER
- ☐ (23136) Practical Guide to Fluid Power 6.95
- ☐ (23167) Pumps 5.95

MATHEMATICS
- ☐ (23112) Practical Math for Everyone
  (2 Vols.) 8.95
  - ☐ Single Volumes sold separately .... ea. 4.95

OUTBOARD MOTORS
- ☐ (23168) Outboard Motors and Boating 4.95

RADIO-TELEVISION-AUDIO
- ☐ (23126) Handbook of Commercial
  Sound Installations 5.95
- ☐ (23128) Practical Guide to Auto
  Radio Repair 4.50
- ☐ (23132) Practical Guide to Servicing
  Electronic Organs 4.95
- ☐ (23161) Radio & Television Library
  (2 Vols.) 11.50
- ☐ (23163) Radiomans Guide 5.95
- ☐ (23162) Television Service Manual 5.95

SHEET METAL
- ☐ (23046) Sheet Metal Workers Handy Book .. 5.00

Prices Subject to Change Without Notice

Name _____

Address _____

City _____ State _____ Zip _____

Occupation _____ Employed by _____

☐ **SAVE SHIPPING CHARGES! Enclose Full Payment
With Coupon and We Pay Shipping Charges.** PRINTED IN USA